Travel phrasebooks collection
«Everything Will Be Okay!»

T&P Books Publishing

PHRASEBOOK

— DANISH —

D1564955

By Andrey Taranov

THE MOST IMPORTANT PHRASES

This phrasebook contains
the most important
phrases and questions
for basic communication
Everything you need
to survive overseas

T&P BOOKS

Phrasebook + 250-word dictionary

English-Danish phrasebook & mini dictionary

By Andrey Taranov

The collection of "Everything Will Be Okay" travel phrasebooks published by T&P Books is designed for people traveling abroad for tourism and business. The phrasebooks contain what matters most - the essentials for basic communication. This is an indispensable set of phrases to "survive" while abroad.

You'll also find a mini dictionary with 250 useful words required for everyday communication - the names of months and days of the week, measurements, family members, and more.

T&P Books Publishing
www.tpbooks.com

ISBN: 978-1-78492-418-8

This book is also available in E-book formats.
Please visit www.tpbooks.com or the major online bookstores.

(

FOREWORD

The collection of "Everything Will Be Okay" travel phrasebooks published by T&P Books is designed for people traveling abroad for tourism and business. The phrasebooks contain what matters most - the essentials for basic communication. This is an indispensable set of phrases to "survive" while abroad.

This phrasebook will help you in most cases where you need to ask something, get directions, find out how much something costs, etc. It can also resolve difficult communication situations where gestures just won't help.

This book contains a lot of phrases that have been grouped according to the most relevant topics. You'll also find a mini dictionary with useful words - numbers, time, calendar, colors...

Take "Everything Will Be Okay" phrasebook with you on the road and you'll have an irreplaceable traveling companion who will help you find your way out of any situation and teach you to not fear speaking with foreigners.

TABLE OF CONTENTS

T&P Books Publishing

PRONUNCIATION

Letter	Danish example	T&P phonetic alphabet	English example
Aa	Afrika, kompas	[æ], [ɑ], [ɑ:]	man, father
Bb	barberblad	[b]	baby, book
Cc	cafe, creme	[k]	clock, kiss
Cc [1]	koncert	[s]	city, boss
Dd	direktør	[d]	day, doctor
Dd [2]	facade	[ð]	weather, together
Ee	belgier	[e], [ə]	medal, elm
Ee [3]	elevator	[ɛ]	man, bad
Ff	familie	[f]	face, food
Gg	mango	[g]	game, gold
Hh	høne, knurhår	[h]	home, have
Ii	kolibri	[i], [i:]	feet, Peter
Jj	legetøj	[j]	yes, New York
Kk	leksikon	[k]	clock, kiss
Ll	leopard	[l]	lace, people
Mm	marmor	[m]	magic, milk
Nn	natur, navn	[n]	name, normal
ng	omfang	[ŋ]	English, ring
nk	punktum	[ŋ]	English, ring
Oo	fortov	[o], [ɔ]	drop, baught
Pp	planteolie	[p]	pencil, private
Qq	sequoia	[k]	clock, kiss
Rr	seriøs	[ʁ]	French (guttural) R
Ss	selskab	[s]	city, boss
Tt	strøm, trappe	[t]	tourist, trip
Uu	blæksprutte	[u:]	pool, room
Vv	børnehave	[ʊ]	vase, winter
Ww	whisky	[w]	vase, winter
Xx	Luxembourg	[ks]	box, taxi
Yy	lykke	[y], [ø]	fuel, eternal
Zz	Venezuela	[s]	city, boss

Letter	Danish example	T&P phonetic alphabet	English example
Ææ	ærter	[ɛ], [ɛː]	habit, bad
Øø	grønsager	[ø], [œ]	church, eternal
Åå	åbent, afgå	[ɔ], [oː]	sun, lucky

Comments

[1] before **e, i**
[2] after a stressed vowel
[3] at the beginning of words

LIST OF ABBREVIATIONS

English abbreviations

ab.	-	about
adj	-	adjective
adv	-	adverb
anim.	-	animate
as adj	-	attributive noun used as adjective
e.g.	-	for example
etc.	-	et cetera
fam.	-	familiar
fem.	-	feminine
form.	-	formal
inanim.	-	inanimate
masc.	-	masculine
math	-	mathematics
mil.	-	military
n	-	noun
pl	-	plural
pron.	-	pronoun
sb	-	somebody
sing.	-	singular
sth	-	something
v aux	-	auxiliary verb
vi	-	intransitive verb
vi, vt	-	intransitive, transitive verb
vt	-	transitive verb

Danish abbreviations

f	-	common gender
f pl	-	common gender plural
i	-	neuter
i pl	-	neuter plural
i, f	-	neuter, common gender
ngn.	-	somebody
pl	-	plural

DANISH PHRASEBOOK

This section contains
important phrases that may
come in handy in various
real-life situations.
The phrasebook will help
you ask for directions, clarify
a price, buy tickets, and
order food at a restaurant

T&P Books Publishing

PHRASEBOOK
CONTENTS

T&P Books Publishing

Excuse me, ...

Undskyld, ...
['ɔnˌskylˀ, ...]

Hello.

Hej.
['hɑj]

Thank you.

Tak.
[tɑk]

Good bye.

Farvel.
[fɑ'vɛl]

Yes.

Ja.
['jæ]

No.

Nej.
[nɑjˀ]

I don't know.

Jeg ved det ikke.
[jɑj ve də 'ekə]

Where? | Where to? | When?

Hvor? | Hvorhen? | Hvornår?
['vɒˀ? | 'vɒˀˌhɛn? | vɒ'nɒˀ?]

I need ...

Jeg har brug for ...
[jɑ hɑˀ 'bʁuˀ fə ...]

I want ...

Jeg vil ...
[jɑj ve ...]

Do you have ...?

Har du ...?
['hɑˀ du ...?]

Is there a ... here?

Er der en ... her?
[æg̊ 'dɛˀg̊ en ... hɛˀg̊?]

May I ...?

Må jeg ...?
[mɔˀ jɑ ...?]

..., please (polite request)

... venligst
[... 'vɛnlist]

I'm looking for ...

Jeg leder efter ...
[jɑ 'le:ðə 'ɛftʌ ...]

restroom

toilet
[toa'lɛt]

ATM

udbetalingsautomat
[uðˀbe'tæˀleŋs ɑwto'mæˀt]

pharmacy (drugstore)

apotek
[ɑpo'teˀk]

hospital

hospital
[hɔspi'tæˀl]

police station

politistation
[poli'ti sta'ço'n]

subway

metro
['me:tʁo]

taxi	**taxi** ['tɑksi]
train station	**togstation** ['tɔw sta'ɕoˀn]

My name is ...	**Mit navn er ...** [mit 'nɑwˀn 'æɐ̯ ...]
What's your name?	**Hvad er dit navn?** ['vað 'æɐ̯ dit nɑwˀn?]
Could you please help me?	**Kan du hjælpe mig?** ['kan du 'jɛlpə mɑj?]
I've got a problem.	**Jeg har fået et problem.** [jɑ hɑˀ fɒˀ et pʁo'bleˀm]
I don't feel well.	**Jeg føler mig dårlig.** [jɑ 'føːlɐ mɑj 'dɒːli]
Call an ambulance!	**Ring efter en ambulance!** ['ʁɛŋə 'ɛftʌ en ɑmbu'lɑŋsə]
May I make a call?	**Må jeg foretage et opkald?** [mɔˀ jɑ 'fɒːɒ̯ˌtæˀ et 'ʌpkalˀ?]

I'm sorry.	**Det er jeg ked af.** [de 'æɐ̯ jɑ 'keðˀ æˀ]
You're welcome.	**Selv tak.** [sɛlˀ tɑk]

I, me	**Jeg, mig** [jɑj, mɑj]
you (inform.)	**du** [du]
he	**han** [han]
she	**hun** [hun]
they (masc.)	**de** [di]
they (fem.)	**de** [di]
we	**vi** [vi]
you (pl)	**I, De** [I, di]
you (sg, form.)	**De** [di]

ENTRANCE	**INDGANG** ['enˌgɑŋˀ]
EXIT	**UDGANG** ['uðˌgɑŋˀ]
OUT OF ORDER	**UDE AF DRIFT** ['uːðə æˀ 'dʁɛft]
CLOSED	**LUKKET** ['lɔkəð]

OPEN	**ÅBEN** [ˈɔːbən]
FOR WOMEN	**TIL KVINDER** [te ˈkvenʌ]
FOR MEN	**TIL MÆND** [te ˈmɛnˀ]

Questions

Where?	**Hvor?** ['vɒˀ?]
Where to?	**Hvorhen?** ['vɒˀˌhɛn?]
Where from?	**Hvorfra?** ['vɒˀˌfʁɑˀ?]
Why?	**Hvorfor?** ['vɔfʌ?]
For what reason?	**Af hvilken grund?** [æˀ 'velkən 'gʁɒnˀ?]
When?	**Hvornår?** [vɒ'nɒˀ?]
How long?	**Hvor længe?** [vɒˀ 'lɛŋə?]
At what time?	**På hvilket tidspunkt?** [pɔ 'velkəð 'tiðspɒŋˀt?]
How much?	**Hvor meget?** [vɒˀ 'maɑð?]
Do you have ...?	**Har du ...?** ['hɑˀ du ...?]
Where is ...?	**Hvor er ...?** [vɒˀ 'æɐ̯ ...?]
What time is it?	**Hvad er klokken?** ['vað 'æɐ̯ 'klʌkən?]
May I make a call?	**Må jeg foretage et opkald?** [mɔˀ ja 'fɒːɒˌtæˀ et 'ʌpkalˀ?]
Who's there?	**Hvem der?** [vɛm 'dɛˀɐ̯?]
Can I smoke here?	**Må jeg ryge her?** [mɔˀ ja 'ʁyːə 'hɛˀɐ̯?]
May I ...?	**Må jeg ...?** [mɔˀ ja ...?]

Needs

I'd like ...	**Jeg vil gerne ...** [jɑj ve 'gæɡnə ...]
I don't want ...	**Jeg ønsker ikke ...** [jɑ 'ønskɡ 'ekə ...]
I'm thirsty.	**Jeg er tørstig.** ['jɑj 'æɡ 'tœɡsti]
I want to sleep.	**Jeg ønsker at sove.** [jɑ 'ønskɡ ʌ 'sɒwə]

I want ...	**Jeg vil ...** [jɑj ve ...]
to wash up	**at vaske** [ʌ 'vaskə]
to brush my teeth	**at børste mine tænder** [ʌ 'bæɡstə 'miːnə 'tɛnʌ]
to rest a while	**at hvile en stund** [ʌ 'viːlə en 'stonʔ]
to change my clothes	**at klæde mig om** [ʌ 'klɛʔ 'mɑj ʌm]

to go back to the hotel	**at gå tilbage til hotellet** [ʌ 'gɔʔ te'bæːjə te ho'tɛlʔəð]
to buy ...	**at købe ...** [ʌ 'køːbə ...]
to go to ...	**at gå til ...** [ʌ 'gɔ te ...]
to visit ...	**at besøge ...** [ʌ be'søʔjə ...]
to meet with ...	**at mødes med ...** [ʌ 'møːðəs mɛ ...]
to make a call	**at foretage et opkald** [ʌ 'fɒːɒˌtæʔ et 'ʌpkalʔ]

I'm tired.	**Jeg er træt.** ['jɑj 'æɡ 'tʁat]
We are tired.	**Vi er trætte.** ['vi 'æɡ 'tʁatə]
I'm cold.	**Jeg fryser.** [jɑ 'fʁyːsʌ]
I'm hot.	**Jeg har det varmt.** [jɑ haʔ de 'vɑʔmt]
I'm OK.	**Jeg er OK.** ['jɑj 'æɡ ɔw'kɛj]

I need to make a call.

Jeg har brug for at foretage et opkald.
[ja hɑ' 'bʁu' fə ʌ 'foːɒˌtæ' et 'ʌpkal']

I need to go to the restroom.

Jeg har brug for at gå på toilettet.
[ja hɑ' 'bʁu' fə ʌ gɔ' pɔ toa'lɛət]

I have to go.

Jeg er nødt til at gå.
['jaj 'æɐ̯ nø't te ʌ gɔ']

I have to go now.

Jeg er nødt til at gå nu.
['jaj 'æɐ̯ nø't te ʌ gɔ' nu]

Asking for directions

Excuse me, ...

Undskyld, ...
['ɔnˌskylˀ, ...]

Where is ...?

Hvor er ...?
[vɒˀ 'æɐ̯ ...?]

Which way is ...?

Hvilken vej er ...?
['velkən 'vajˀ 'æɐ̯ ...?]

Could you help me, please?

Er du sød at hjælpe mig?
[æɐ̯ du 'søðˀ ʌ 'jɛlpə majˀ]

I'm looking for ...

Jeg leder efter ...
[ja 'leːðə 'ɛftʌ ...]

I'm looking for the exit.

Jeg leder efter udgangen.
[ja 'leːðə 'ɛftʌ 'uðˌgaŋən]

I'm going to ...

Jeg har tænkt mig at ...
[ja haˀ 'tɛŋkt maj ʌ ...]

Am I going the right way to ...?

Går jeg den rigtige vej til ...?
[gɒˀ ja dən 'ʁɛgtiə vajˀ te ...?]

Is it far?

Er det langt væk?
[æɐ̯ de 'laŋˀt vɛk?]

Can I get there on foot?

Kan jeg komme derhen til fods?
['kanˀ ja 'kʌmə 'dɛˀɐ̯'hɛn te 'foˀðs?]

Can you show me on the map?

Kan du vise mig på kortet?
['kan du 'viːsə maj pɒ 'kɒːtəð?]

Show me where we are right now.

Vis mig, hvor vi er lige nu.
['viˀs maj, vɒˀ vi 'æɐ̯ 'liːə nu]

Here

Her
['hɛˀɐ̯]

There

Der
[dɛˀɐ̯]

This way

Denne vej
['dɛnə vajˀ]

Turn right.

Drej til højre.
[dʁajˀ te 'hʌjʁʌ]

Turn left.

Drej til venstre.
[dʁajˀ te 'vɛnstʁʌ]

first (second, third) turn

første (anden, tredje) vej
['fœɐ̯stə ('anən, 'tʁɛðjə) vajˀ]

to the right

til højre
[te 'hʌjʁʌ]

to the left

til venstre
[te 'vɛnstʁʌ]

Go straight ahead.

Gå ligeud.
['gɔˀ 'liːəˈuðˀ]

Signs

WELCOME!	**VELKOMMEN!** ['vɛlˌkʌmˀən]
ENTRANCE	**INDGANG** ['enˌgɑŋˀ]
EXIT	**UDGANG** ['uðˌgɑŋˀ]
PUSH	**SKUB** [skɔb]
PULL	**TRÆK** ['tʁak]
OPEN	**ÅBEN** ['ɔ:bən]
CLOSED	**LUKKET** ['lɔkəð]
FOR WOMEN	**TIL KVINDER** [te 'kvenʌ]
FOR MEN	**TIL MÆND** [te 'mɛnˀ]
GENTLEMEN, GENTS (m)	**MÆND** [mɛnˀ]
WOMEN (f)	**KVINDER** ['kvenʌ]
DISCOUNTS	**UDSALG** ['uðˌsalˀ]
SALE	**RESTSALG** ['ʁast ˌsalˀ]
FREE	**GRATIS** ['gʁɑ:tis]
NEW!	**NYT!** [nyt]
ATTENTION!	**OBS!** [ʌbs]
NO VACANCIES	**ALT OPTAGET** ['alˀt 'ʌpˌtæˀəð]
RESERVED	**RESERVERET** [ʁɛsæɐ'veˀʌð]
ADMINISTRATION	**ADMINISTRATION** [aðministʁɑ'ɕoˀn]
STAFF ONLY	**KUN PERSONALE** [kɔn pæɐso'næ:lə]

BEWARE OF THE DOG!	**PAS PÅ HUNDEN!** [pas pɔ 'hunən]
NO SMOKING!	**RYGNING FORBUDT!** ['ʁyːnen fʌ'byˀd]
DO NOT TOUCH!	**RØR IKKE!** ['ʁœˀɐ̯ 'ekə]
DANGEROUS	**FARLIGT** ['fɑːlit]
DANGER	**FARE** ['fɑːɑ]
HIGH VOLTAGE	**STÆRKSTRØM** ['stæɐ̯k 'stʁœmˀ]
NO SWIMMING!	**SVØMNING FORBUDT!** ['svœmnen fʌ'byˀt]

OUT OF ORDER	**UDE AF DRIFT** ['uːðə æˀ 'dʁɛft]
FLAMMABLE	**BRANDFARLIG** ['bʁɑnˌfɑːli]
FORBIDDEN	**FORBUDT** [fʌ'byˀt]
NO TRESPASSING!	**ADGANG FORBUDT!** ['aðˌgɑŋˀ fʌ'byˀð]
WET PAINT	**VÅD MALING** ['vɔˀð 'mæːlen]

CLOSED FOR RENOVATIONS	**LUKKET PGA. RENOVERING** ['lɔkəð pɔˀ 'gʁɔnˀ a ʁɛno've'ɐ̯en]
WORKS AHEAD	**ARBEJDE FORUDE** ['ɑːˌbɑjˀdə 'fɔːˌuːðə]
DETOUR	**OMKØRSEL** [ɔm'køɐ̯səl]

Transportation. General phrases

plane	**fly** [fly']
train	**tog** ['tɔ'w]
bus	**bus** [bus]
ferry	**færge** ['fæɐ̯wə]
taxi	**taxi** ['tɑksi]
car	**bil** [bi'l]

schedule	**køreplan** ['køːʌˌplæˀn]
Where can I see the schedule?	**Hvor kan jeg se køreplanen?** [vɒˀ kan ja seˀ 'køːʌˌplæˀnən?]
workdays (weekdays)	**hverdage** ['væɐ̯ˌdæˀə]
weekends	**weekender** ['wiːˌkɛndʌ]
holidays	**helligdage** ['hɛliˌdæˀə]

DEPARTURE	**AFGANG** ['awˌgaŋˀ]
ARRIVAL	**ANKOMST** ['anˌkʌmˀst]
DELAYED	**FORSINKET** [fəˈsenˀkəð]
CANCELLED	**AFLYST** ['awˌlyˀst]

next (train, etc.)	**næste** ['nɛstə]
first	**første** ['fœɐ̯stə]
last	**sidste** ['sistə]

When is the next ...?	**Hvornår er den næste ...?** [vɒˈnɒˀ 'æɐ̯ dən 'nɛstə ...?]
When is the first ...?	**Hvornår er den første ...?** [vɒˈnɒˀ 'æɐ̯ dən 'fœɐ̯stə ...?]

When is the last ...?

Hvornår er den sidste ...?
[vɒˈnɒˀ ˈæɡ dən ˈsistə ...?]

transfer (change of trains, etc.)

skift
[ˈskift]

to make a transfer

at skifte
[ʌ ˈskiftə]

Do I need to make a transfer?

Behøver jeg at skifte?
[beˈhøˀvə ˈjɑj ʌ ˈskiftə?]

Buying tickets

Where can I buy tickets?	**Hvor kan jeg købe billetter?** [vɒˀ kan ja 'køːbə bi'lɛtʌ?]
ticket	**billet** [bi'lɛt]
to buy a ticket	**at købe en billet** [ʌ 'køːbə en bi'lɛt]
ticket price	**billetpris** [bi'lɛtˌpʁiˀs]

Where to?	**Hvorhen?** ['vɒˀˌhɛn?]
To what station?	**Til hvilken station?** [te 'velkən staˈɕoˀn?]
I need ...	**Jeg har brug for ...** [ja haˀ 'bʁuˀ fə ...]
one ticket	**én billet** [en bi'lɛt]
two tickets	**to billetter** [toˀ bi'lɛtʌ]
three tickets	**tre billetter** ['tʁɛˀ bi'lɛtʌ]

one-way	**enkelt** ['ɛŋˀkəlt]
round-trip	**retur** [ʁɛ'tuɐ̯ˀ]
first class	**første klasse** ['fœɐ̯stə 'klasə]
second class	**anden klasse** ['anən 'klasə]

today	**i dag** [i 'dæˀ]
tomorrow	**i morgen** [i 'mɒːɒn]
the day after tomorrow	**i overmorgen** [i 'ɒwʌˌmɒːɒn]
in the morning	**om morgenen** [ʌm 'mɒːɒnən]
in the afternoon	**om eftermiddagen** [ʌm 'ɛftʌmeˌdæˀən]
in the evening	**om aftenen** [ʌm 'aftənən]

aisle seat

gangplads
['gaŋplas]

window seat

vinduesplads
['vendus 'plas]

How much?

Hvor meget?
[vɒ' 'maað?]

Can I pay by credit card?

Kan jeg betale med kreditkort?
['kan' ja be'tæ'lə mɛ kʁɛ'dit kɒ:t?]

Bus

bus	**bus** [bus]
intercity bus	**rutebil** ['ʁuːtə‿biˀl]
bus stop	**busstoppested** ['busˌstɒpəstɛð]
Where's the nearest bus stop?	**Hvor er det nærmeste busstoppested?** [vɒˀ 'æg̊ de 'næɐ̯məstə 'busˌstɒpəstɛð?]
number (bus ~, etc.)	**nummer** ['nɔmˀʌ]
Which bus do I take to get to ...?	**Hvilken bus skal jeg tage for at komme til ...?** ['velkən bus skalˀ ja 'tæˀə fə ʌ 'kʌmə te ...?]
Does this bus go to ...?	**Kører denne bus til ...?** ['køːɐ̯ 'dɛnə bus te ...?]
How frequent are the buses?	**Hvor hyppigt kører busserne?** [vɒˀ 'hypit 'køːɐ̯ 'busɐ̯nə?]
every 15 minutes	**hvert kvarter** ['vɛˀɐ̯t kvɑ'teˀɐ̯]
every half hour	**hver halve time** ['vɛɐ̯ halˀvə 'tiːmə]
every hour	**hver time** ['vɛɐ̯ 'tiːmə]
several times a day	**flere gange om dagen** ['fleːʌ 'gɑŋə ʌm 'dæˀən]
... times a day	**... gange om dagen** [... 'gɑŋə ʌm 'dæˀən]
schedule	**køreplan** ['køːʌˌplæˀn]
Where can I see the schedule?	**Hvor kan jeg se køreplanen?** [vɒˀ kan ja seˀ 'køːʌˌplæˀnən?]
When is the next bus?	**Hvornår kører den næste bus?** [vɒ'nɒˀ 'køːɐ̯ dən 'nɛstə bus?]
When is the first bus?	**Hvornår kører den første bus?** [vɒ'nɒˀ 'køːɐ̯ dən 'fœɐ̯stə bus?]
When is the last bus?	**Hvornår kører den sidste bus?** [vɒ'nɒˀ 'køːɐ̯ dən 'sistə bus?]

stop	**stop** ['stʌp]
next stop	**næste stop** ['nɛstə 'stʌp]
last stop (terminus)	**sidste stop** ['sistə 'stʌp]
Stop here, please.	**Stop her, tak.** ['stʌp 'hɛ'ɐ̯, tɑk]
Excuse me, this is my stop.	**Undskyld, det er mit stop.** ['ɔnˌskyl', de 'æɐ̯ mit 'stʌp]

Train

train	**tog** ['tɔˀw]
suburban train	**regionaltog** [ʁɛgjoˈnæˀl tɔˀw]
long-distance train	**intercitytog** [entʌˈsiti tɔˀw]
train station	**togstation** ['tɔw staˈɕoˀn]
Excuse me, where is the exit to the platform?	**Undskyld, hvor er udgangen til perronen?** ['ɔnˌskylˀ, vɒˀ 'æɐ̯ 'uðˌgɑŋən te paˈʁʌŋən?]

Does this train go to ...?	**Kører dette tog til ...?** ['køːɐ̯ 'dɛtə tɔˀw te ...?]
next train	**næste tog** ['nɛstə 'tɔˀw]
When is the next train?	**Hvornår afgår det næste tog?** [vɒˈnɒˀ 'awˌgɔˀ de 'nɛstə tɔˀw?]
Where can I see the schedule?	**Hvor kan jeg se køreplanen?** [vɒˀ kan ja seˀ 'køːʌˌplæˀnən?]
From which platform?	**Fra hvilken perron?** [ˌfʁɑˀ 'velkən paˈʁʌŋ?]
When does the train arrive in ...?	**Hvornår ankommer toget til ...?** [vɒˈnɒˀ 'anˌkʌmʌ 'tɔˀwəð te ...?]

Please help me.	**Vær sød at hjælpe mig.** ['vɛɐ̯ˀ 'søðˀ ʌ 'jɛlpə mɑj]
I'm looking for my seat.	**Jeg leder efter min plads.** [ja 'leːðə 'ɛftʌ min plas]
We're looking for our seats.	**Vi leder efter vores pladser.** ['vi 'leːðə 'ɛftʌ 'vɒɒs 'plasʌ]
My seat is taken.	**Min plads er taget.** [min 'plas 'æɐ̯ 'tæəð]
Our seats are taken.	**Vore pladser er taget.** ['vɒːɒ 'plasʌ 'æɐ̯ 'tæəð]

I'm sorry but this is my seat.	**Jeg beklager, men dette er min plads.** [ja beˈklæˀjə, mɛn 'dɛtə 'æɐ̯ min 'plas]
Is this seat taken?	**Er denne plads taget?** [æɐ̯ 'dɛnə plas 'tæəð?]
May I sit here?	**Må jeg sidde her?** [mɔˀ ja 'seðə 'hɛˀɐ̯?]

On the train. Dialogue (No ticket)

Ticket, please.

Billet, tak.
[bi'lɛt, tɑk]

I don't have a ticket.

Jeg har ikke nogen billet.
[jɑ hɑˀ 'ekə 'noən bi'lɛt]

I lost my ticket.

Jeg har mistet min billet.
[jɑ hɑˀ 'mestəð min bi'lɛt]

I forgot my ticket at home.

Jeg har glemt min billet derhjemme.
[jɑ hɑˀ 'glɛmt min bi'lɛt dɑ'jɛmə]

You can buy a ticket from me.

Du kan købe en billet af mig.
[du kan 'kø:bə en bi'lɛt æˀ mɑj]

You will also have to pay a fine.

**Du bliver også nødt
til at betale en bøde.**
[du 'bliɐ̯ˀ ʌsə nøˀt
te ʌ be'tæˀlə en 'bø:ðə]

Okay.

OK.
[ɔw'kɛj]

Where are you going?

Hvor skal du hen?
[vɒˀ skalˀ du hɛn?]

I'm going to ...

Jeg har tænkt mig at ...
[jɑ hɑˀ 'tɛŋkt mɑj ʌ ...]

How much? I don't understand.

Hvor meget? Jeg forstår det ikke.
[vɒˀ 'mɑɑð? jɑ fə'stɒ de 'ekə]

Write it down, please.

Skriv det ned, tak.
['skʁiwˀ de neðˀ, tɑk]

Okay. Can I pay with a credit card?

OK. Kan jeg betale med kreditkort?
[ɔw'kɛj. kan jɑ be'tæˀlə mɛ kʁɛ'dit kɒ:t?]

Yes, you can.

Ja, det kan du godt.
['jæ, de kan du 'gʌt]

Here's your receipt.

Her er din kvittering.
['hɛˀɐ̯ 'æɐ̯ din kvi'teˀɐ̯eŋ]

Sorry about the fine.

Undskyld bøden.
['ɔnˌskylˀ 'bø:ðən]

That's okay. It was my fault.

Det er OK. Det var min skyld.
[de 'æɐ̯ ɔw'kɛj. de vɑ min skylˀ]

Enjoy your trip.

Nyd turen.
[nyð 'tuɐ̯ˀn]

Taxi

taxi	**taxi** ['taksi]
taxi driver	**taxichauffør** ['taksi ɕo'fø'ɐ̯]
to catch a taxi	**at få fat i en taxi** [ʌ fɔ' fat i en 'taksi]
taxi stand	**taxiholdeplads** ['taksi 'hʌlə‚plas]
Where can I get a taxi?	**Hvor kan jeg finde en taxi?** [vɒ' kan jaj 'fenə en 'taksi?]
to call a taxi	**at ringe efter en taxi** [ʌ 'ʁɛŋə 'ɛftʌ en 'taksi]
I need a taxi.	**Jeg har brug for en taxi.** [ja ha' 'bʁu' fə en 'taksi]
Right now.	**Lige nu.** ['li:ə 'nu]
What is your address (location)?	**Hvad er din adresse?** ['vað 'æɐ̯ din a'dʁasə?]
My address is ...	**Min adresse er ...** [min a'dʁasə 'æɐ̯ ...]
Your destination?	**Hvor skal du hen?** [vɒ' skal' du hɛn?]
Excuse me, ...	**Undskyld, ...** ['ɔn‚skyl', ...]
Are you available?	**Er du ledig?** [æɐ̯ du 'le:ði?]
How much is it to get to ...?	**Hvor meget koster det at komme til ...?** [vɒ' 'maɑð 'kʌstɐ de ʌ 'kʌmə te ...?]
Do you know where it is?	**Ved du, hvor det er?** [ve du, vɒ' de 'æɐ̯?]
Airport, please.	**Lufthavnen, tak.** ['lɔft‚haw'nən, tak]
Stop here, please.	**Stop her, tak.** ['stʌp 'hɛ'ɐ̯, tak]
It's not here.	**Det er ikke her.** [de 'æɐ̯ 'ekə 'hɛ'ɐ̯]
This is the wrong address.	**Det er den forkerte adresse.** [de 'æɐ̯ dən fə'keɐ̯'tə a'dʁasə]

Turn left.

Drej til venstre.
[dʁɑjˀ te ˈvɛnstʁʌ]

Turn right.

Drej til højre.
[dʁɑjˀ te ˈhʌjʁʌ]

How much do I owe you?

Hvor meget skylder jeg dig?
[vɒˀ ˈmɑɑð ˈskylə jɑ dɑjˀ?]

I'd like a receipt, please.

Jeg vil gerne have en kvittering, tak.
[jɑj ve ˈgæɐ̯nə hæˀ en kviˈteˀɐ̯eŋ, tɑk]

Keep the change.

Behold resten.
[beˈhʌlˀ ˈʁastən]

Would you please wait for me?

Vil du venligst vente på mig?
[ˈve du ˈvɛnlist ˈvɛntə pɔ mɑjˀ?]

five minutes

fem minutter
[fɛmˀ meˈnutʌ]

ten minutes

ti minutter
[ˈtiˀ meˈnutʌ]

fifteen minutes

femten minutter
[ˈfɛmtən meˈnutʌ]

twenty minutes

tyve minutter
[ˈtyːvə meˈnutʌ]

half an hour

en halv time
[en ˈhalˀ ˈtiːmə]

Hotel

Hello.
Hej.
['hɑj]

My name is ...
Mit navn er ...
[mit 'nɑwˀn 'æɐ̯ ...]

I have a reservation.
Jeg har en reservation.
[jɑ haˀ en ʁɛsæɐ̯va'ɕoˀn]

I need ...
Jeg har brug for ...
[jɑ haˀ 'bʁuˀ fə ...]

a single room
et enkeltværelse
[et 'ɛŋˀkəlt͜væɐ̯ʌlsə]

a double room
et dobbeltværelse
[et 'dʌbəlt 'væɐ̯ʌlsə]

How much is that?
Hvor meget bliver det?
[vɒˀ 'mɑɑð 'bliˀ de?]

That's a bit expensive.
Det er lidt dyrt.
[de 'æɐ̯ lit 'dyɐ̯ˀt]

Do you have anything else?
Har du nogen andre muligheder?
['haˀ du 'noən 'andʁʌ 'muːliˌheðˀʌ?]

I'll take it.
Det tager jeg.
[de 'tæˀɐ̯ jɑj]

I'll pay in cash.
Jeg betaler kontant.
[jɑ be'tæˀlʌ kɔn'tanˀt]

I've got a problem.
Jeg har fået et problem.
[jɑ haˀ fɔˀ et pʁo'bleˀm]

My ... is broken.
Mit ... er gået i stykker.
[mit ... 'æɐ̯ 'gɔːəð 'støkʌ]

My ... is out of order.
Mit ... virker ikke.
[mit ... 'viɐ̯kʌ 'ekə]

TV
TV
['teˀˌveˀ]

air conditioner
klimaanlæg
['kliːma'anˌlɛˀg]

tap
hane
['hæːnə]

shower
bruser
['bʁuːsʌ]

sink
vask
['vask]

safe
pengeskab
['pɛŋəˌskæˀb]

door lock	**dørlås** ['dœɡlɔˀs]
electrical outlet	**stikkontakt** ['stek kɔn'tɑkt]
hairdryer	**hårtørrer** ['hɔːˌtœɡʌ]

I don't have ...	**Jeg har ikke nogen ...** [jɑ hɑˀ 'ekə 'noən ...]
water	**vand** ['vanˀ]
light	**lys** ['lyˀs]
electricity	**elektricitet** [elɛktʁisi'teˀt]

Can you give me ...?	**Kan du give mig ...?** ['kan du giˀ mɑj ...?]
a towel	**et håndklæde** [ed 'hʌnˌklɛːðə]
a blanket	**et tæppe** [ed 'tɛpə]
slippers	**hjemmesko** ['jɛməˌskoˀ]
a robe	**en kåbe** [en 'kɔːbə]
shampoo	**shampoo** ['ɕæːmˌpuː]
soap	**sæbe** ['sɛːbə]

I'd like to change rooms.	**Jeg vil gerne skifte værelse.** [jɑj ve 'gæɡnə 'skiftə 'væɡʌlsə]
I can't find my key.	**Jeg kan ikke finde min nøgle.** [jɑ kan 'ekə 'fenə min 'nʌjlə]
Could you open my room, please?	**Kunne du låse op til mit værelse?** ['kunə du 'lɔːsə ʌp te mit 'væɡʌlsə?]
Who's there?	**Hvem der?** [vɛm 'dɛˀɡ?]
Come in!	**Kom ind!** [kʌmˀ enˀ]
Just a minute!	**Et øjeblik!** [ed 'ʌjə'blek]
Not right now, please.	**Ikke lige nu, tak.** ['ekə 'liːə nu, tɑk]

Come to my room, please.	**Kom til mit værelse, tak.** [kʌmˀ te mit 'væɡʌlsə, tɑk]
I'd like to order food service.	**Jeg vil gerne bestille roomservice.** [jɑj ve 'gæɡnə be'stelˀə 'ʁuːmˌsœːvis]
My room number is ...	**Mit værelsesnummer er ...** [mɪt 'væɡʌlsə'nɔmˀʌ 'æɡ ...]

I'm leaving ...

Jeg forlader ...
[jɑ fə'læ'ðə ...]

We're leaving ...

Vi forlader ...
['vi fə'læ'ðə ...]

right now

lige nu
['li:ə 'nu]

this afternoon

i eftermiddag
[I 'ɛftʌmeˌdæ']

tonight

i aften
[i 'ɑftən]

tomorrow

i morgen
[i 'mɒːɒn]

tomorrow morning

i morgen tidlig
[i 'mɒːɒn 'tiðli]

tomorrow evening

i morgen aften
[i 'mɒːɒn 'ɑftən]

the day after tomorrow

i overmorgen
[i 'ɒwʌˌmɒːɒn]

I'd like to pay.

Jeg vil gerne betale.
[jɑj ve 'gæɡnə be'tæ'lə]

Everything was wonderful.

Alt var vidunderligt.
['al't vɑ við'ɔn'ʌlit]

Where can I get a taxi?

Hvor kan jeg finde en taxi?
[vɒ' kan jɑj 'fenə en 'tɑksi?]

Would you call a taxi for me, please?

Vil du ringe efter en taxi for mig, tak?
['ve du 'ʁɛŋə 'ɛftʌ en 'tɑksi fə mɑj, tɑk?]

Restaurant

Can I look at the menu, please? **Kan jeg se menuen?**
['kan' jɑ se' me'nyən?]

Table for one. **Bord til én.**
['bo'g̈ te 'en]

There are two (three, four) of us. **Vi er to (tre, fire).**
[vi 'æg̈ to' ('tʁɛ', 'fi'ʌ)]

Smoking **Rygning**
['ʁy:nen]

No smoking **Rygning forbudt**
['ʁy:nen fʌ'by'd]

Excuse me! (addressing a waiter) **Undskyld!**
['ɔnˌskyl']

menu **menu**
[me'ny]

wine list **vinkort**
['vi:nˌkɒ:t]

The menu, please. **Menuen, tak.**
[me'nyən, tɑk]

Are you ready to order? **Er du klar til at bestille?**
[æg̈ du klɑ' te ʌ be'stel'ə?]

What will you have? **Hvad vil du have?**
['vað ve du hæ'?]

I'll have … **Jeg vil gerne have …**
[jɑj ve 'gæg̈nə hæ' …]

I'm a vegetarian. **Jeg er vegetar.**
['jɑj 'æg̈ vegə'tɑ']

meat **kød**
['køð]

fish **fisk**
['fesk]

vegetables **grøntsager**
['gʁɶntˌsæ'jʌ]

Do you have vegetarian dishes? **Har du vegetarretter?**
['hɑ' du vegə'tɑ'ʁatə?]

I don't eat pork. **Jeg spiser ikke svinekød.**
[jɑ 'spi:sg̈ 'ekə 'svi:nə'køð]

He /she/ doesn't eat meat. **Han /hun/ spiser ikke kød.**
[han /hun/ 'spi:sg̈ 'ekə 'køð]

I am allergic to … **Jeg er allergisk over for …**
['jɑj 'æg̈ a'læg̈'gisk 'ɒw'ʌ fə …]

Would you please bring me ...	**Er du sød at give mig ...** [æɡ du 'søð' ʌ 'gi' maj ...]
salt | pepper | sugar	**salt | peber | sukker** ['sal'ṭ | 'pewʌ | 'sɔkʌ]
coffee | tea | dessert	**kaffe | te | dessert** ['kɑfə | te' | de'sɛɡ't]
water | sparkling | plain	**vand | med brus | uden brus** ['van' | mɛ 'bʁu's | 'uðən 'bʁu's]
a spoon | fork | knife	**en ske | gaffel | kniv** [en ske' | 'gɑfəl | 'kniw']
a plate | napkin	**en tallerken | serviet** [en ta'læɡkən | sæɡvi'ɛt]

Enjoy your meal!	**Nyd dit måltid!** [nyð dit 'mʌl̩tið']
One more, please.	**En til, tak.** [en te, tɑk]
It was very delicious.	**Det var meget lækkert.** [de vɑ 'mɑɑð 'lɛkʌt]

check | change | tip	**regningen | byttepenge | drikkepenge** ['ʁɑjneŋən | 'bytə,pɛŋə | 'dʁɛkə,pɛŋə]
Check, please. (Could I have the check, please?)	**Regningen, tak.** ['ʁɑjneŋən, tɑk]
Can I pay by credit card?	**Kan jeg betale med kreditkort?** ['kan' ja be'tæ'lə mɛ kʁɛ'dit kɒːt?]
I'm sorry, there's a mistake here.	**Undskyld, men der er en fejl her.** ['ɔn,skyl', mɛn 'dɛ'ɡ 'æɡ en 'faj'l 'hɛ'ɡ]

Shopping

Can I help you?	**Kan jeg hjælpe?** ['kan' ja 'jɛlpə?]
Do you have …?	**Har du …?** ['hɑ' du …?]
I'm looking for …	**Jeg leder efter …** [ja 'le:ðə 'ɛftʌ …]
I need …	**Jeg har brug for …** [ja hɑ' 'bʁu' fə …]

I'm just looking.	**Jeg kigger bare.** [ja 'kigʌ 'bɑ:ɑ]
We're just looking.	**Vi kiggede bare.** ['vi 'kigəðə 'bɑ:ɑ]
I'll come back later.	**Jeg kommer tilbage senere.** [ja 'kʌmʌ te'bæ:jə 'se'nʌʌ]
We'll come back later.	**Vi kommer tilbage senere.** ['vi 'kʌmʌ te'bæ:jə 'se'nʌʌ]
discounts	sale	**rabatter	udsalg** [ʁɑ'batʌ	'uð‚sal']

Would you please show me …	**Vil du være sød at vise mig …** ['ve du 'vɛɐ̯' søð' ʌ 'vi:sə mɑj …]
Would you please give me …	**Vil du give mig …** ['ve du gi' mɑj …]
Can I try it on?	**Kan jeg prøve det på?** ['kan' ja 'pʁœ:wə de pɔ'?]
Excuse me, where's the fitting room?	**Undskyld, hvor er prøverummet?** ['ɔn‚skyl', vɒ' 'æɐ̯ 'pʁœ:wə 'ʁɔməð?]
Which color would you like?	**Hvilken farve vil du have?** ['velkən 'fɑ:və ve du hæ'?]
size	length	**størrelse	længde** ['stœɐ̯ʌlsə	'lɛŋ'də]
How does it fit?	**Hvordan passer det?** [vɒ'dan 'pasʌ de?]

How much is it?	**Hvor meget bliver det?** [vɒ' 'maɑð 'bliɐ̯' de?]
That's too expensive.	**Det er for dyrt.** [de 'æɐ̯ fə 'dyɐ̯'t]
I'll take it.	**Det tager jeg.** [de 'tæ'ɐ̯ jɑj]
Excuse me, where do I pay?	**Undskyld, hvor kan jeg betale?** ['ɔn‚skyl', vɒ' kan' ja be'tæ'lə?]

Will you pay in cash or credit card?	**Vil du betale kontant eller med kreditkort?** ['ve du be'tæ'lə kɔn'tan't mɛ kʁɛ'dit kɒ:t?]
In cash | with credit card	**Kontant | med kreditkort** [kɔn'tan't | mɛ kʁɛ'dit kɒ:t]

Do you want the receipt?	**Vil du have kvitteringen?** ['ve du hæ' kvi'te'ɡeŋən?]
Yes, please.	**Ja, tak.** ['jæ, tɑk]
No, it's OK.	**Nej, det er OK.** [nɑj', de 'æɡ ɔw'kɛj]
Thank you. Have a nice day!	**Tak. Hav en dejlig dag!** [tɑk. 'hɑ' en 'dɑjli 'dæ']

In town

Excuse me, please.
Undskyld mig.
['ɔnˌskyl' mɑj]

I'm looking for ...
Jeg leder efter ...
[ja 'le:ðə 'ɛftʌ ...]

the subway
metroen
['me:tʁoən]

my hotel
mit hotel
[mit ho'tɛl']

the movie theater
biografen
[bio'gʁɑ'fən]

a taxi stand
en taxiholdeplads
[en 'tɑksi 'hʌləˌplas]

an ATM
en udbetalingsautomat
[en uð'be'tæ'leŋs ɑwto'mæ't]

a foreign exchange office
et vekselkontor
[et 'vɛksəl kɔn'to'ɐ]

an internet café
en internetcafé
[en 'entʌˌnɛt ka'fe']

... street
... gade
[... 'gæ:ðə]

this place
dette sted
['dɛtə 'stɛð]

Do you know where ... is?
Ved du, hvor ... er?
[ve du, vɒ' ... 'æɐ?]

Which street is this?
Hvilken gade er dette?
['velkən 'gæ:ðə 'æɐ 'dɛtə?]

Show me where we are right now.
Vis mig, hvor vi er lige nu.
['vi's mɑj, vɒ' vi 'æɐ 'li:ə nu]

Can I get there on foot?
Kan jeg komme derhen til fods?
['kan' ja 'kʌmə 'dɛ'ɐ'hɛn te 'fo'ðs?]

Do you have a map of the city?
Har du et kort over byen?
['hɑ' du et 'kɒːt 'ɒw'ʌ 'byən?]

How much is a ticket to get in?
Hvor meget koster en billet for at komme ind?
[vɒ' 'mɑɑð 'kʌstɐ en bi'lɛt fə ʌ 'kʌmə 'en'?]

Can I take pictures here?
Må jeg tage billeder her?
[mɔ' ja tæ' 'beləðʌ 'hɛ'ɐ?]

Are you open?
Har du åbent?
['hɑ' du 'ɔ:bənt?]

When do you open?

Hvornår åbner du?
[vɒ'nɒˀ 'ɔːbnʌ du?]

When do you close?

Hvornår lukker du?
[vɒ'nɒˀ 'lɔkɐ du?]

Money

money	**penge** ['pɛŋə]
cash	**kontanter** [kɔn'tanˀtʌ]
paper money	**sedler** ['sɛðˀlʌ]
loose change	**småmønter** [ˌsmʌ'mønˀtʌ]
check | change | tip	**regningen | byttepenge | drikkepenge** ['ʁɑjnɐŋən | 'bytəˌpɛŋə | 'dʁɛkəˌpɛŋə]

credit card	**kreditkort** [kʁɛ'dit kɒːt]
wallet	**tegnebog** ['tajnəbɔˀw]
to buy	**at købe** [ʌ 'køːbə]
to pay	**at betale** [ʌ be'tæˀlə]
fine	**bøde** ['bøːðə]
free	**gratis** ['gʁɑːtis]

Where can I buy ...?	**Hvor kan jeg købe ...?** [vɒˀ kan ja 'køːbə ...?]
Is the bank open now?	**Har banken åbent nu?** ['haˀ 'baŋkən 'ɔːbənt nu?]
When does it open?	**Hvornår åbner den?** [vɒˀnɒˀ 'ɔːbnʌ dɛnˀ?]
When does it close?	**Hvornår lukker den?** [vɒˀnɒˀ 'lɔkɐ dɛnˀ?]

How much?	**Hvor meget?** [vɒˀ 'maɑðˀ?]
How much is this?	**Hvor meget bliver det?** [vɒˀ 'maɑðˀ 'bliɐˀ de?]
That's too expensive.	**Det er for dyrt.** [de 'æɐ̯ fə 'dyɐ̯ˀt]

Excuse me, where do I pay?	**Undskyld, hvor kan jeg betale?** ['ɔnˌskylˀ, vɒˀ kan ja be'tæˀlə?]
Check, please.	**Regningen, tak.** ['ʁɑjnɐŋən, tak]

Can I pay by credit card? | **Kan jeg betale med kreditkort?**
['kanˀ ja be'tæˀlə mɛ kʁɛ'dit kɒ:t?]

Is there an ATM here? | **Er der en udbetalingsautomat her?**
[æɐ̯ 'dɛˀɐ̯ en uð'be'tæˀleŋs awto'mæˀt 'hɛˀɐ̯?]

I'm looking for an ATM. | **Jeg leder efter en udbetalingsautomat.**
[ja 'le:ðə 'ɛftʌ en uð'be'tæˀleŋs awto'mæˀt]

I'm looking for a foreign exchange office. | **Jeg leder efter et vekselkontor.**
[ja 'le:ðə 'ɛftʌ et 'vɛksəl kɔn'to'ɐ̯]

I'd like to change ... | **Jeg vil gerne veksle ...**
[jaj ve 'gæɐ̯nə 'vɛkslə ...]

What is the exchange rate? | **Hvad er vekselkursen?**
['vað 'æɐ̯ 'vɛksəl 'kuɐ̯ˀsən]

Do you need my passport? | **Har du brug for mit pas?**
['hɑˀ du 'bʁuˀ fə mit 'pas?]

Time

What time is it?	**Hvad er klokken?** ['vað 'æɐ̯ 'klʌkən?]
When?	**Hvornår?** [vɒ'nɒˀ?]
At what time?	**På hvilket tidspunkt?** [pɔ 'velkəð 'tiðspɒŋˀt?]
now | later | after ...	**nu | senere | efter ...** ['nu | 'seˀnʌʌ | 'ɛftʌ ...]
one o'clock	**klokken et** ['klʌkən et]
one fifteen	**kvart over et** ['kvɑːt 'ɒwˀʌ et]
one thirty	**halv to** ['halˀ 'toˀ]
one forty-five	**kvart i to** ['kvɑːt i 'toˀ]

one | two | three	**et | to | tre** [ed | toˀ | tʁɛˀ]
four | five | six	**fire | fem | seks** ['fiˀʌ | fɛmˀ | 'sɛks]
seven | eight | nine	**syv | otte | ni** ['sywˀ | 'ɔːtə | niˀ]
ten | eleven | twelve	**ti | elleve | tolv** ['tiˀ | 'ɛlvə | tʌlˀ]

in ...	**om ...** [ʌm ...]
five minutes	**fem minutter** [fɛmˀ me'nutʌ]
ten minutes	**ti minutter** ['tiˀ me'nutʌ]
fifteen minutes	**femten minutter** ['fɛmtən me'nutʌ]
twenty minutes	**tyve minutter** ['tyːvə me'nutʌ]
half an hour	**en halv time** [en 'halˀ 'tiːmə]
an hour	**en time** [en 'tiːmə]
in the morning	**om morgenen** [ʌm 'mɒːɒnən]
early in the morning	**tidligt om morgenen** ['tiðlit ʌm 'mɒːɒnən]

this morning	**her til morgen** ['hɛˀɐ te 'mɒːɒn]
tomorrow morning	**i morgen tidlig** [i 'mɒːɒn 'tiðli]

in the middle of the day	**midt på dagen** ['met pɔ 'dæˀən]
in the afternoon	**om eftermiddagen** [ʌm 'ɛftʌme‚dæˀən]
in the evening	**om aftenen** [ʌm 'ɑftənən]
tonight	**i aften** [i 'ɑftən]

at night	**om natten** [ʌm 'nɛtn]
yesterday	**i går** [i 'gɒˀ]
today	**i dag** [i 'dæˀ]
tomorrow	**i morgen** [i 'mɒːɒn]
the day after tomorrow	**i overmorgen** [i 'ɒwʌmɒːɒn]

What day is it today?	**Hvilken dag er det i dag?** ['velkən 'dæˀ 'æɐ de i 'dæˀ?]
It's ...	**Det er ...** [de 'æɐ ...]
Monday	**Mandag** ['manˀda]
Tuesday	**tirsdag** ['tiɐˀsda]
Wednesday	**onsdag** ['ɔnˀsda]

Thursday	**torsdag** ['tɒˀsda]
Friday	**Fredag** ['fʁɛˀda]
Saturday	**Lørdag** ['lœɐda]
Sunday	**søndag** ['sœnˀda]

Greetings. Introductions

Hello.	**Hej.** ['haj]
Pleased to meet you.	**Glad for at møde dig.** ['glað fə ʌ 'mø:ðə 'daj]
Me too.	**Det samme her.** [de 'samə 'hɛˀɐ̯]
I'd like you to meet ...	**Jeg vil gerne have at du møder ...** [jaj ve 'gæɐ̯nə hæˀ ʌ du 'mø:ðə ...]
Nice to meet you.	**Rart at møde dig.** ['ʁaˀt ʌ 'mø:ðə daj]
How are you?	**Hvordan har du det?** [vɒ'dan haˀ du de?]
My name is ...	**Mit navn er ...** [mit 'nawˀn 'æɐ̯ ...]
His name is ...	**Hans navn er ...** [hans 'nawˀn 'æɐ̯ ...]
Her name is ...	**Hendes navn er ...** ['henəs 'nawˀn 'æɐ̯ ...]
What's your name?	**Hvad hedder du?** ['vað 'heðʌ du?]
What's his name?	**Hvad hedder han?** ['vað 'heðʌ han?]
What's her name?	**Hvad hedder hun?** ['vað 'heðʌ hun?]
What's your last name?	**Hvad er dit efternavn?** ['vað 'æɐ̯ did 'ɛftʌˌnawˀn?]
You can call me ...	**Du kan ringe til mig ...** [du kan 'ʁɛŋə te maj ...]
Where are you from?	**Hvor er du fra?** [vɒˀ 'æɐ̯ du fʁaˀ]
I'm from ...	**Jeg er fra ...** ['jaj 'æɐ̯ fʁaˀ ...]
What do you do for a living?	**Hvad arbejder du med?** ['vað 'aːˌbajˀdʌ du mɛ?]
Who is this?	**Hvem er det?** [vɛm 'æɐ̯ de?]
Who is he?	**Hvem er han?** [vɛm 'æɐ̯ han?]
Who is she?	**Hvem er hun?** [vɛm 'æɐ̯ hun?]

Who are they?	**Hvem er de?** [vɛm 'æɐ̯ di?]
This is ...	**Dette er ...** ['dɛtə 'æɐ̯ ...]
my friend (masc.)	**min ven** [min 'vɛn]
my friend (fem.)	**min veninde** [min vɛn'enə]
my husband	**min mand** [min 'manˀ]
my wife	**min kone** [min 'koːnə]

my father	**min far** [min 'fɑː]
my mother	**min mor** [min 'moɐ̯]
my brother	**min bror** [min 'bʁoɐ̯]
my sister	**min søster** [min 'søstʌ]
my son	**min søn** [min 'sœn]
my daughter	**min datter** [min 'datʌ]

This is our son.	**Dette er vores søn.** ['dɛtə 'æɐ̯ 'vɒɒs 'sœn]
This is our daughter.	**Dette er vores datter.** ['dɛtə 'æɐ̯ 'vɒɒs 'datʌ]
These are my children.	**Dette er mine børn.** ['dɛtə 'æɐ̯ 'miːnə 'bœɐ̯ˀn]
These are our children.	**Dette er vores børn.** ['dɛtə 'æɐ̯ 'vɒɒs 'bœɐ̯ˀn]

Farewells

Good bye!

Farvel!
[fɑ'vɛl]

Bye! (inform.)

Hej hej!
['hɑj 'hɑj]

See you tomorrow.

Ses i morgen.
['seˀs i 'mɒːɒn]

See you soon.

Vi ses snart.
['vi 'seˀs 'snɑˀt]

See you at seven.

Vi ses klokken syv.
['vi 'seˀs 'klʌkən 'syw']

Have fun!

Have det sjovt!
['hɑˀ de 'ɕɒwd]

Talk to you later.

Vi snakkes ved senere.
['vi 'snɑkəs ve 'seˀnʌʌ]

Have a nice weekend.

Ha' en dejlig weekend.
[ha en 'dɑjli 'wiːˌkɛnd]

Good night.

Godnat.
[go'nad]

It's time for me to go.

Det er på tide at jeg smutter.
[de 'æɡ pɒ 'tiːðə ʌ jɑ 'smutə]

I have to go.

Jeg bliver nødt til at gå.
[jɑ 'bliɡˀ nøˀt te ʌ 'ɡɔˀ]

I will be right back.

Jeg kommer straks tilbage.
[jɑ 'kʌmʌ 'stʁaks te'bæːjə]

It's late.

Det er sent.
[de 'æɡ 'seˀnt]

I have to get up early.

Jeg er nødt til at stå tidligt op.
['jɑj 'æɡ nøˀt te ʌ 'stɔˀ 'tiðlit 'ʌp]

I'm leaving tomorrow.

Jeg rejser i morgen.
[jɑ 'ʁɑjsə i 'mɒːɒn]

We're leaving tomorrow.

Vi rejser i morgen.
['vi 'ʁɑjsə i 'mɒːɒn]

Have a nice trip!

Hav en dejlig tur!
['hɑˀ en 'dɑjli 'tuɡˀ]

It was nice meeting you.

Det var rart at møde dig.
[de vɑ 'ʁɑˀt ʌ 'møːðə 'dɑj]

It was nice talking to you.

Det var rart at tale med dig.
[de vɑ 'ʁɑˀt ʌ 'tæːlə mɛ 'dɑj]

Thanks for everything.

Tak for alt.
[tɑk fə 'alˀt]

I had a very good time.

Jeg nød tiden sammen.
[ja nøːð 'tiðən 'samˀən]

We had a very good time.

Vi nød virkeligt tiden sammen.
['vi nøːð 'virkəlit 'tiðən 'samˀən]

It was really great.

Det var virkeligt godt.
[de va 'virkəlit 'gʌt]

I'm going to miss you.

Jeg kommer til at savne dig.
[ja 'kʌmʌ te ʌ 'sawnə 'daj]

We're going to miss you.

Vi kommer til at savne dig.
['vi 'kʌmʌ te ʌ 'sawnə 'daj]

Good luck!

Held og lykke!
['hɛlˀ ʌ 'løkə]

Say hi to ...

Sig hej til ...
['saj 'haj te ...]

Foreign language

I don't understand.	**Jeg forstår det ikke.** [ja fə'stɐ̯ de 'ekə]
Write it down, please.	**Skriv det ned, tak.** ['skʁiw' de neð', tak]
Do you speak ...?	**Taler du ...?** ['tæːlʌ du ...?]
I speak a little bit of ...	**Jeg taler en lille smule ...** [ja 'tæːlʌ en 'lilə 'smuːlə ...]
English	**engelsk** ['ɛŋ'əlsk]
Turkish	**tyrkisk** ['tyɐ̯kisk]
Arabic	**arabisk** [a'ʁɑ'bisk]
French	**fransk** ['fʁɑn'sk]
German	**tysk** ['tysk]
Italian	**italiensk** [ital'jɛ'nsk]
Spanish	**spansk** ['span'sk]
Portuguese	**portugisisk** [pɒtu'gi'sisk]
Chinese	**kinesisk** [ki'ne'sisk]
Japanese	**japansk** [ja'pæ'nsk]
Can you repeat that, please.	**Kan du gentage det, tak.** ['kan du 'gɛn̩tæ' de, tak]
I understand.	**Jeg forstår.** [ja fə'stɐ̯]
I don't understand.	**Jeg forstår det ikke.** [ja fə'stɐ̯ de 'ekə]
Please speak more slowly.	**Tal langsommere.** ['tal 'laŋ̩sʌm'əʌ]
Is that correct? (Am I saying it right?)	**Er det rigtigt?** [æɐ̯ de 'ʁɛgtit?]
What is this? (What does this mean?)	**Hvad er dette?** ['vað 'æɐ̯ 'dɛtə?]

Apologies

Excuse me, please.
Undskyld mig.
['ɔnˌskylˀ majl]

I'm sorry.
Det er jeg ked af.
[de 'æɐ̯ ja 'keðˀ æˀ]

I'm really sorry.
Jeg er virkelig ked af det.
['jaj 'æɐ̯ 'viɐ̯keli 'keðˀ æˀ de]

Sorry, it's my fault.
Beklager, det er min skyld.
[be'klæˀjə, de 'æɐ̯ min 'skylˀ]

My mistake.
Min fejl.
[min 'fajˀl]

May I ...?
Må jeg ...?
[mɔˀ ja ...?]

Do you mind if I ...?
Har du noget imod, hvis jeg ...?
['haˀ du 'noːəð i'moðˀ, 'ves jaj ...?]

It's OK.
Det er OK.
[de 'æɐ̯ ɔw'kɛj]

It's all right.
Det er OK.
[de 'æɐ̯ ɔw'kɛj]

Don't worry about it.
Tag dig ikke af det.
['tæˀ 'daj 'ekə æˀ de]

Agreement

Yes. | **Ja.**
['jæ]

Yes, sure. | **Ja, helt sikkert.**
['jæ, 'heˀlt 'sekʌt]

OK (Good!) | **Godt!**
['gʌt]

Very well. | **Meget godt.**
['mɑɑð 'gʌt]

Certainly! | **Bestemt!**
[be'stɛmˀt]

I agree. | **Jeg er enig.**
['jɑj 'æɐ̯ 'eːni]

That's correct. | **Det er korrekt.**
[de 'æɐ̯ ko'ʁakt]

That's right. | **Det er rigtigt.**
[de 'æɐ̯ 'ʁɛgtit]

You're right. | **Du har ret.**
[du hɑˀ 'ʁat]

I don't mind. | **Jeg har ikke noget imod det.**
[jɑ hɑˀ 'ekə 'noːəð i'moðˀ de]

Absolutely right. | **Helt korrekt.**
['heˀlt ko'ʁakt]

It's possible. | **Det er muligt.**
[de 'æɐ̯ 'muːlit]

That's a good idea. | **Det er en god idé.**
[de 'æɐ̯ en 'goðˀ i'deˀ]

I can't say no. | **Jeg kan ikke sige nej.**
[jɑ kan 'ekə 'si: 'nɑjˀ]

I'd be happy to. | **Jeg ville være glad for.**
[jɑj 'vilə 'vɛɐ̯ˀ 'glað fə]

With pleasure. | **Med glæde.**
[mɛ 'glɛːðə]

Refusal. Expressing doubt

No.	**Nej.** [nɑjˀ]
Certainly not.	**Bestemt ikke.** [be'stɛmˀt 'ekə]
I don't agree.	**Jeg er ikke enig.** ['jɑj 'æɐ̯ 'ekə 'eːni]
I don't think so.	**Jeg tror det ikke.** [jɑ 'tʁoˀɐ̯ de 'ekə]
It's not true.	**Det er ikke sandt.** [de 'æɐ̯ 'ekə 'sant]
You are wrong.	**Du tager fejl.** [du 'tæˀɐ̯ 'fɑjˀl]
I think you are wrong.	**Jeg tror, du tager fejl.** [jɑ 'tʁoˀɐ̯, du 'tæˀɐ̯ 'fɑjˀl]
I'm not sure.	**Jeg er ikke sikker.** ['jɑj 'æɐ̯ 'ekə 'sekʌ]
It's impossible.	**Det er umuligt.** [de 'æɐ̯ u'muˀlit]
Nothing of the kind (sort)!	**Overhovedet ikke!** [ɒwʌ'hoːədəð 'ekə]
The exact opposite.	**Det stik modsatte.** [de 'stek 'moð‚satə]
I'm against it.	**Jeg er imod det.** ['jɑj 'æɐ̯ i'moðˀ de]
I don't care.	**Jeg er ligeglad.** ['jɑj 'æɐ̯ 'liːə‚glað]
I have no idea.	**Jeg aner det ikke.** ['jɑj 'æːnə de 'ekə]
I doubt it.	**Jeg tvivler på det.** [jɑ 'tviwlə pɔˀ de]
Sorry, I can't.	**Undskyld, jeg kan ikke.** ['ɔn‚skylˀ, jɑ kanˀ 'ekə]
Sorry, I don't want to.	**Undskyld, jeg ønsker ikke at.** ['ɔn‚skylˀ, jɑ 'ønskɐ 'ekə ʌ]
Thank you, but I don't need this.	**Tak, men jeg har ikke brug for dette.** [tak, mɛn jɑ 'hɑˀ 'ekə 'bʁuˀ fə 'dɛtə]
It's getting late.	**Det bliver sent.** [de 'bliɐ̯ˀ 'seˀnt]

I have to get up early.

Jeg er nødt til at stå tidligt op.
['jɑj 'æɐ̯ nøˀt te ʌ 'stɔˀ 'tiðlit ʌp]

I don't feel well.

Jeg føler mig dårlig.
[jɑ 'føːlɐ̯ mɑj 'dɒːli]

Expressing gratitude

Thank you.	**Tak.** [tɑk]
Thank you very much.	**Mange tak.** ['maŋə 'tɑk]
I really appreciate it.	**Jeg sætter virkeligt pris på det.** [ja sɛtʌ 'viɐ̯kəlit 'pʁiˀs pɔˀ de]
I'm really grateful to you.	**Jeg er dig virkeligt taknemmelig.** ['jaj 'æɐ̯ dɑ 'viɐ̯kəlit tɑk'nɛmˀəli]
We are really grateful to you.	**Vi er dig virkeligt taknemmelige.** ['vi 'æɐ̯ dɑ 'viɐ̯kəlit tɑk'nɛmˀəliə]

Thank you for your time.	**Tak for din tid.** [tɑk fə din 'tiðˀ]
Thanks for everything.	**Tak for alt.** [tɑk fə 'alˀt]
Thank you for ...	**Tak for ...** [tɑk fə ...]
your help	**din hjælp** [din 'jɛlˀp]
a nice time	**en dejlig tid** [en 'dɑjli 'tiðˀ]

a wonderful meal	**et vidunderligt måltid** [ed við'ɔnˀʌlit 'mʌlˌtiðˀ]
a pleasant evening	**en hyggelig aften** [en 'hygəli 'aften]
a wonderful day	**en vidunderlig dag** [en við'ɔnˀʌli 'dæˀ]
an amazing journey	**en fantastisk rejse** [en fan'tastisk 'ʁajsə]

Don't mention it.	**Glem det.** ['glɛm de]
You are welcome.	**Du er velkommen.** [du 'æɐ̯ 'vɛlˌkʌmˀən]
Any time.	**Når som helst.** ['nɒˀ sʌm 'hɛlˀst]
My pleasure.	**Intet problem.** ['entəð pʁo'bleˀm]
Forget it.	**Glem det.** ['glɛm de]
Don't worry about it.	**Tag dig ikke af det.** ['tæˀ 'dɑj 'ekə æˀ de]

Congratulations. Best wishes

Congratulations!
Til lykke!
[te 'løkə]

Happy birthday!
Tillykke med fødselsdagen!
[tə'løkə mɛ 'føsəls‚dæ'ən]

Merry Christmas!
Glædelig jul!
['glɛ:ðəli 'ju'l]

Happy New Year!
Godt Nytår!
['gʌt 'nyt‚ɒ']

Happy Easter!
God påske!
['goð' 'pɔ:skə]

Happy Hanukkah!
Glædelig Hanukkah!
['glɛ:ðəli 'hanuka]

I'd like to propose a toast.
Jeg vil gerne udbringe en skål.
[jɑj ve 'gæɐ̯nə 'uð‚bʁɛŋ'ə en 'skɔ'l]

Cheers!
Skål!
['skɔ'l]

Let's drink to …!
Lad os skåle for …!
[lað ʌs 'skɔ:lə fə …!]

To our success!
Til vores succes!
[te 'vɒɒs syk'se]

To your success!
Til din succes!
[te din syk'se]

Good luck!
Held og lykke!
['hɛl' ʌ 'løkə]

Have a nice day!
Hav en dejlig dag!
['ha' en 'dɑjli 'dæ']

Have a good holiday!
Hav en god ferie!
['ha' en 'goð' 'feɐ̯'iə]

Have a safe journey!
Har en sikker rejse!
['ha' en 'sekʌ 'ʁɑjsə!]

I hope you get better soon!
Jeg håber du får det bedre snart!
[jɑ 'hɔ:bʌ du fɒ' de 'bɛðʁʌ 'snɑ't]

Socializing

Why are you sad?	**Hvorfor er du ked af det?** ['vɔfʌ 'æɐ̯ du 'keð' æ' de?]
Smile! Cheer up!	**Smil! Op med humøret!** ['smiˀl! ʌb mɛ hu'mø'ɐ̯əð]
Are you free tonight?	**Er du fri i aften?** [æɐ̯ du 'fʁiˀ i 'ɑftən?]
May I offer you a drink?	**Må jeg tilbyde dig en drink?** [mɔˀ jɑ 'tel̩ˌbyˀðə 'dɑj en 'dʁiŋk?]
Would you like to dance?	**Kunne du tænke dig at danse?** ['kunə du 'tɛŋkə·dɑj ʌ 'dansə?]
Let's go to the movies.	**Lad os gå i biografen.** [lɑð ʌs 'gɔˀ i bio'gʁɑˀfən]
May I invite you to …?	**Må jeg invitere dig til …?** [mɔˀ jɑ envi'teˀʌ dɑ te …?]
a restaurant	**en restaurant** [en ʁɛsto'ʁɑŋ]
the movies	**biografen** [bio'gʁɑˀfən]
the theater	**teatret** [te'æˀtʁəð]
go for a walk	**at gå en tur** [ʌ 'gɔˀ en 'tuɐ̯ˀ]
At what time?	**På hvilket tidspunkt?** [pɔ 'velkəð 'tiðspɔŋˀt?]
tonight	**i aften** [i 'ɑftən]
at six	**klokken seks** ['klʌkən 'sɛks]
at seven	**klokken syv** ['klʌkən 'sywˀ]
at eight	**klokken otte** ['klʌkən 'ɔːtə]
at nine	**klokken ni** ['klʌkən 'niˀ]
Do you like it here?	**Kan du lide det her?** ['kan du 'liːðə de 'hɛˀɐ̯?]
Are you here with someone?	**Er du her med nogen?** [æɐ̯ du 'hɛˀɐ̯ mɛ 'noən?]
I'm with my friend.	**Jeg er sammen med min ven.** ['jɑj 'æɐ̯ 'samˀən mɛ min 'vɛn]

I'm with my friends.	**Jeg er sammen med mine venner.** ['jɑj 'æɐ̯ 'sɑm'ən mɛ'mi:nə 'vɛnʌ]
No, I'm alone.	**Nej, jeg er alene.** [nɑj', jɑ 'æɐ̯ a'le:nə]

Do you have a boyfriend?	**Har du en kæreste?** ['hɑ' du en 'kæɐ̯ʌstə?]
I have a boyfriend.	**Jeg har en kæreste.** [jɑ hɑ' en 'kæɐ̯ʌstə]
Do you have a girlfriend?	**Har du en kæreste?** ['hɑ' du en 'kæɐ̯ʌstə?]
I have a girlfriend.	**Jeg har en kæreste.** [jɑ hɑ' en 'kæɐ̯ʌstə]

Can I see you again?	**Kan jeg se dig igen?** ['kan' jɑ se' dɑj i'gɛn?]
Can I call you?	**Kan jeg ringe til dig?** ['kan' jɑ 'ʁɛŋə te dɑj?]
Call me. (Give me a call.)	**Ring til mig.** ['ʁɛŋə te mɑj]
What's your number?	**Hvad er dit nummer?** ['vað 'æɐ̯ dit 'nɔm'ʌ?]
I miss you.	**Jeg savner dig.** [jɑ 'sɑwnɐ dɑj]

You have a beautiful name.	**Du har et smukt navn.** [du hɑ' et 'smɔkt 'nɑw'n]
I love you.	**Jeg elsker dig.** ['jɑj 'ɛlskʌ dɑj]
Will you marry me?	**Vil du gifte dig med mig?** ['ve du 'giftə 'dɑj mɛ mɑj?]

You're kidding!	**Du spøger!** [du 'spø:jə]
I'm just kidding.	**Jeg spøger.** [jɑ 'spø:jə]

Are you serious?	**Mener du det alvorligt?** ['me:nʌ du de al'vɒ'lit?]
I'm serious.	**Jeg mener det alvorligt.** [jɑ 'me:nʌ de al'vɒ'lit]
Really?!	**Virkeligt?!** ['viɐ̯kəlit?!]
It's unbelievable!	**Det er utroligt!** [de 'æɐ̯ u'tʁo'lit]
I don't believe you.	**Jeg tror dig ikke.** [jɑ 'tʁo'ɐ̯ 'dɑj 'ekə]

I can't.	**Jeg kan ikke.** [jɑ kan 'ekə]
I don't know.	**Jeg ved det ikke.** [jɑj ve de 'ekə]

I don't understand you.	**Jeg forstår dig ikke.** [ja fe'stɐ daj 'ekə]
Please go away.	**Gå din vej.** ['gɔˀ din 'vajˀ]
Leave me alone!	**Lad mig være!** [lað maj 'vɛɐ̯ˀ]

I can't stand him.	**Jeg kan ikke fordrage ham.** [ja kan 'ekə fe'dʁɑˀwə ham]
You are disgusting!	**Du er modbydelig!** [du 'æɐ̯ moð'byðˀəli]
I'll call the police!	**Jeg ringer til politiet!** [ja 'ʁɛŋʌ te poli'tiˀəð]

Sharing impressions. Emotions

I like it.
Jeg kan lide det.
[ja kan 'li:ðə de]

Very nice.
Meget fint.
['maɑð 'fi'nt]

That's great!
Det er godt!
[de 'æɐ̯ 'gʌt]

It's not bad.
Det er ikke dårligt.
[de 'æɐ̯ 'ekə 'dɒ:lit]

I don't like it.
Jeg kan ikke lide det.
[ja kan 'ekə 'li:ðə de]

It's not good.
Det er ikke godt.
[de 'æɐ̯ 'ekə 'gʌt]

It's bad.
Det er dårligt.
[de 'æɐ̯ 'dɒ:lit]

It's very bad.
Det er meget dårligt.
[de 'æɐ̯ 'maɑð 'dɒ:lit]

It's disgusting.
Det er ulækkert.
[de 'æɐ̯ 'uˌlɛkʌt]

I'm happy.
Jeg er glad.
['jaj 'æɐ̯ 'glað]

I'm content.
Jeg er tilfreds.
['jaj 'æɐ̯ te'fʁɛs]

I'm in love.
Jeg er forelsket.
['jaj 'æɐ̯ fə'ɛl'skəð]

I'm calm.
Jeg er rolig.
['jaj 'æɐ̯ 'ʁo:li]

I'm bored.
Jeg keder mig.
[ja 'ke:ðʌ maj]

I'm tired.
Jeg er træt.
['jaj 'æɐ̯ 'tʁat]

I'm sad.
Jeg er ked af det.
['jaj 'æɐ̯ 'keð' æ' de]

I'm frightened.
Jeg er bange.
['jaj 'æɐ̯ 'baŋə]

I'm angry.
Jeg er vred.
['jaj 'æɐ̯ 'vʁɛð']

I'm worried.
Jeg er bekymret.
['jaj 'æɐ̯ be'køm'ʁʌð]

I'm nervous.
Jeg er nervøs.
['jaj 'æɐ̯ næɐ̯'vø's]

I'm jealous. (envious)

Jeg er misundelig.
['jɑj 'æɐ̯ mis'ɔn'əli]

I'm surprised.

Jeg er overrasket.
['jɑj 'æɐ̯ 'ɒwʌˌʁɑskəð]

I'm perplexed.

Jeg er forvirret.
['jɑj 'æɐ̯ fʌ'viɐ̯'ʌð]

Problems. Accidents

I've got a problem.	**Jeg har fået et problem.** [ja haˀ fɔˀ et pʁoˈbleˀm]
We've got a problem.	**Vi har fået et problem.** [ˈvi haˀ ˈfɔˀ et pʁoˈbleˀm]
I'm lost.	**Jeg forstår ikke.** [ja fəˈstɐ ˈekə]
I missed the last bus (train).	**Jeg kom for sent til den sidste bus (tog).** [ja ˈkʌmˀ fə ˈseˀnt te dən ˈsistə bus (ˈtɔˀw)]
I don't have any money left.	**Jeg har ikke nogen penge tilbage.** [ja haˀ ˈekə ˈnoən ˈpɛŋə teˈbæːjə]

I've lost my ...	**Jeg har mistet min ...** [ja haˀ ˈmestəð min ...]
Someone stole my ...	**Nogen stjal mit ...** [ˈnoən ˈstjæˀl mit ...]
passport	**pas** [ˈpas]
wallet	**tegnebog** [ˈtajnəbɔˀw]
papers	**papirer** [paˈpiːɐˀ]
ticket	**billet** [biˈlɛt]
money	**penge** [ˈpɛŋə]
handbag	**håndtaske** [ˈhʌnˈtaskə]
camera	**kamera** [ˈkæˀməʁa]
laptop	**laptop** [ˈlapˌtʌp]
tablet computer	**tablet computer** [ˈtablɛt kʌmˈpjuːtʌ]
mobile phone	**mobiltelefon** [moˈbil teləˈfoˀn]

Help me!	**Hjælp mig!** [ˈjɛlˀp maj]
What's happened?	**Hvad er der sket?** [ˈvað ˈæɐ̯ ˈdɛˀɐ̯ ˈskeˀð?]
fire	**brand** [ˈbʁɑnˀ]

shooting	**skyderi** [skyðʌ'ʁi²]
murder	**mord** ['moˀɐ̯]
explosion	**eksplosion** [ɛksplo'ɕoˀn]
fight	**kamp** ['kɑmˀp]

Call the police!	**Ring til politiet!** ['ʁɛŋə te poli'tiˀəð]
Please hurry up!	**Vær sød at skynde dig!** ['vɛɐ̯ˀ 'søðˀ ʌ 'skønə 'dɑj]
I'm looking for the police station.	**Jeg leder efter politistationen.** [ja 'leːðə 'ɛftʌ poli'ti sta'ɕoˀnən]
I need to make a call.	**Jeg har brug for at foretage et opkald.** [ja haˀ 'bʁuˀ fə ʌ 'foːˌtæˀ et 'ʌpkalˀ]
May I use your phone?	**Må jeg bruge din telefon?** [mɔˀ ja 'bʁuːə din telə'foˀn?]

I've been ...	**Jeg er blevet ...** ['jaj 'æɐ̯ 'blewəð ...]
mugged	**overfaldet** ['ɒwʌˌfalˀəð]
robbed	**røvet** ['ʁœwəð]
raped	**voldtaget** ['vʌlˌtæˀəð]
attacked (beaten up)	**angrebet** ['anˌgʁɛˀbəð]

Are you all right?	**Er du okay?** [æɐ̯ du ɔw'kɛj?]
Did you see who it was?	**Så du, hvem det var?** ['sɔˀ du, vɛm de 'vɑ?]
Would you be able to recognize the person?	**Ville du være i stand til at genkende personen?** ['vilə du 'vɛɐ̯ˀ i 'stan te ʌ 'gɛnˌkɛnˀə pæɐ̯'soˀnən?]
Are you sure?	**Er du sikker?** ['æɐ̯ du 'sekʌ?]

Please calm down.	**Fald til ro.** ['falˀ te 'ʁoˀ]
Take it easy!	**Tag det roligt!** ['tæˀ de 'ʁoːlit]
Don't worry!	**Det går nok!** [de gɒˀ 'nʌk]
Everything will be fine.	**Alt vil være OK.** ['alˀt ve 'vɛɐ̯ˀ ɔw'kɛj]
Everything's all right.	**Alt er okay.** ['alˀt 'æɐ̯ ɔw'kɛj]

Come here, please.

Kom her.
[kʌmˀ 'hɛˀɐ̯]

I have some questions for you.

Jeg har nogle spørgsmål til dig.
[jɑ hɑˀ 'noːlə 'sbœɐ̯s͵mɔˀl te 'dɑj]

Wait a moment, please.

Vent et øjeblik.
['vɛnt et 'ʌjə͵blek]

Do you have any I.D.?

Har du nogen ID?
['hɑˀ du 'noən 'iˀˀdeˀ?]

Thanks. You can leave now.

Tak. Du kan gå nu.
[tɑk. du kan 'gɔˀ nu]

Hands behind your head!

Hænderne bag hovedet!
['hɛnˀʌnə 'bæˀ 'hoːðəð]

You're under arrest!

Du er anholdt!
[du 'æɐ̯ 'an͵hʌlt]

Health problems

Please help me.	**Vær sød at hjælpe mig.** ['vɛɐ̯' 'søð' ʌ 'jɛlpə mɑj]
I don't feel well.	**Jeg føler mig dårlig.** [jɑ 'fø:lɐ mɑj 'dɒ:li]
My husband doesn't feel well.	**Min mand føler sig dårlig.** [min 'man' 'fø:lɐ sɑj 'dɒ:li]
My son ...	**Min søn ...** [min 'sœn ...]
My father ...	**Min far ...** [min 'fɑ: ...]
My wife doesn't feel well.	**Min kone føler sig dårlig.** [min 'ko:nə 'fø:lɐ sɑj 'dɒ:li]
My daughter ...	**Min datter ...** [min 'datʌ ...]
My mother ...	**Min mor ...** [min 'moɐ̯ ...]
I've got a ...	**Jeg har fået ...** [jɑ hɑ' fɒ' ...]
headache	**hovedpine** ['ho:əð‚pi:nə]
sore throat	**ondt i halsen** ['ɔnt i 'hal'sən]
stomach ache	**mavepine** ['mæ:və 'pi:nə]
toothache	**tandpine** ['tan‚pi:nə]
I feel dizzy.	**Jeg føler mig svimmel.** [jɑ 'fø:lɐ mɑj 'svem'əl]
He has a fever.	**Han har feber.** [han hɑ' 'fe'bʌ]
She has a fever.	**Hun har feber.** [hun hɑ' 'fe'bʌ]
I can't breathe.	**Jeg kan ikke få vejret.** [jɑ kan 'ekə fɒ' 'vɑj‚ʁat]
I'm short of breath.	**Jeg er forpustet.** ['jɑj 'æɐ̯ fə'pu'stəð]
I am asthmatic.	**Jeg er astmatiker.** ['jɑj 'æɐ̯ ast'mæ'tikʌ]
I am diabetic.	**Jeg er diabetiker.** ['jɑj 'æɐ̯ dia'be'tikʌ]

I can't sleep.	**Jeg kan ikke sove.** [ja kan 'ekə 'sɒwə]
food poisoning	**madforgiftning** ['maðfʌˌgiftneŋ]

It hurts here.	**Det gør ondt her.** [de 'gœɐ̯ ɔnt 'hɛˀɐ̯]
Help me!	**Hjælp mig!** ['jɛlˀp maj]
I am here!	**Jeg er her!** ['jaj 'æɐ̯ 'hɛˀɐ̯]
We are here!	**Vi er her!** ['vi 'æɐ̯ 'hɛˀɐ̯]
Get me out of here!	**Få mig ud herfra!** ['fɔˀ maj 'uðˀ 'hɛˀɐ̯ˌfʁɑˀ]
I need a doctor.	**Jeg har brug for en læge.** [ja haˀ 'bʁuˀ fə en 'lɛːjə]
I can't move.	**Jeg kan ikke bevæge sig.** [ja kan 'ekə be'vɛˀjə 'saj]
I can't move my legs.	**Jeg kan ikke bevæge mine ben.** [ja kan 'ekə be'vɛˀjə 'miːnə 'beˀn]

I have a wound.	**Jeg har et sår.** [ja haˀ et 'sɒˀ]
Is it serious?	**Er det alvorligt?** [æɐ̯ de al'vɒˀlit?]
My documents are in my pocket.	**Mine papirer ligger i min lomme.** ['miːnə pa'piːɐ̯ˀ 'legʌ i min 'lʌmə]
Calm down!	**Tag det roligt!** ['tæˀ de 'ʁoːlit]
May I use your phone?	**Må jeg bruge din telefon?** [mɔˀ ja 'bʁuːə din tele'foˀn?]

Call an ambulance!	**Ring efter en ambulance!** ['ʁɛŋə 'ɛftʌ en ambu'laŋsə]
It's urgent!	**Det haster!** [de 'hastə]
It's an emergency!	**Det er en nødsituation!** [de 'æɐ̯ en 'nød sitwa'ɕoˀn]
Please hurry up!	**Vær sød at skynde dig!** ['vɛɐ̯ˀ 'søðˀ ʌ 'skønə 'daj]
Would you please call a doctor?	**Vil du venligst ringe til en læge?** ['ve du 'vɛnlist 'ʁɛŋə te en 'lɛːjə?]
Where is the hospital?	**Hvor er hospitalet?** [vɒˀ 'æɐ̯ hɔspi'tæˀləð?]

How are you feeling?	**Hvordan har du det?** [vɒ'dan haˀ du de?]
Are you all right?	**Er du okay?** [æɐ̯ du ɔw'kɛj?]
What's happened?	**Hvad er der sket?** ['vað 'æɐ̯ 'dɛˀɐ̯ 'skeˀð?]

I feel better now.

Jeg har det bedre nu.
[ja ha' de 'bɛðʁʌ 'nu]

It's OK.

Det er OK.
[de 'æɡ̊ ɔw'kɛj]

It's all right.

Det er OK.
[de 'æɡ̊ ɔw'kɛj]

At the pharmacy

pharmacy (drugstore)

apotek
[ɑpo'teˀk]

24-hour pharmacy

døgnåbent apotek
['dʌjˀn 'ɔːbənt ɑpo'teˀk]

Where is the closest pharmacy?

Hvor er det nærmeste apotek?
[vɒˀ 'æɐ̯ de 'næɐ̯məstə ɑpo'teˀk?]

Is it open now?

Holder det åbent nu?
['hʌlʌ de 'ɔːbənt 'nu?]

At what time does it open?

Hvornår åbner det?
[vɒ'nɒˀ 'ɔːbnʌ de?]

At what time does it close?

Hvornår lukker det?
[vɒ'nɒˀ 'lɔkɐ̯ de?]

Is it far?

Er det langt væk?
[æɐ̯ de 'lɑŋˀt vɛk?]

Can I get there on foot?

Kan jeg komme derhen til fods?
['kanˀ ja 'kʌmə 'dɛˀɐ̯'hɛn te 'foˀðs?]

Can you show me on the map?

Kan du vise mig på kortet?
['kan du 'viːsə maj pɔ 'kɒːtəð?]

Please give me something for ...

Kan du give mig noget for ...
['kan du giˀ maj 'noːəð fə ...]

a headache

hovedpine
['hoːəðˌpiːnə]

a cough

hoste
['hoːstə]

a cold

forkølelse
[fʌ'køˀləlsə]

the flu

influenza
[enflu'ɛnsa]

a fever

feber
['feˀbʌ]

a stomach ache

ondt i maven
['ɔnt i 'mæːvən]

nausea

kvalme
['kvalmə]

diarrhea

diarré
[dia'ʁɛˀ]

constipation

forstoppelse
[fʌ'stʌpəlsə]

pain in the back

rygsmerter
['ʁœg 'smæɐ̯tə]

chest pain	**brystsmerter** ['bʁœst 'smæɐ̯tə]
side stitch	**sidesting** ['si:ðə 'steŋˀ]
abdominal pain	**mavesmerter** ['mæ:və 'smæɐ̯tə]

pill	**pille** ['pelə]
ointment, cream	**salve, creme** ['salvə, 'kʁɛˀm]
syrup	**sirup** ['siˀʁɔp]
spray	**spray** ['spʁɛj]
drops	**dråber** ['dʁɔ:bʌ]

You need to go to the hospital.	**Du er nødt til at tage på hospitalet.** [du 'æɐ̯ 'nøˀt te ʌ tæˀ pɔ hɔspi'tæˀləð]
health insurance	**sygesikring** ['sy:ə‚sekʁɛŋ]
prescription	**recept** [ʁɛ'sɛpt]
insect repellant	**mygge-afskrækker** ['mygə-'ɑw‚skʁakʌ]
Band Aid	**hæfteplaster** ['hɛftə 'plastʌ]

The bare minimum

Excuse me, ...	**Undskyld, ...** [ˈɔnˌskylˀ, ...]
Hello.	**Hej.** [ˈhɑj]
Thank you.	**Tak.** [tɑk]
Good bye.	**Farvel.** [fɑˈvɛl]
Yes.	**Ja.** [ˈjæ]
No.	**Nej.** [nɑjˀ]
I don't know.	**Jeg ved det ikke.** [jɑj ve de ˈekə]
Where? | Where to? | When?	**Hvor? | Hvorhen? | Hvornår?** [ˈvɒˀ? | ˈvɒˀˌhɛn? | vɒˈnɒˀ?]

I need ...	**Jeg har brug for ...** [jɑ hɑˀ ˈbʁuˀ fə ...]
I want ...	**Jeg vil ...** [jɑj ve ...]
Do you have ...?	**Har du ...?** [ˈhɑˀ du ...?]
Is there a ... here?	**Er der en ... her?** [æɐ̯ ˈdɛˀɐ̯ en ... hɛˀɐ̯?]
May I ...?	**Må jeg ...?** [mɔˀ jɑ ...?]
..., please (polite request)	**... venligst** [... ˈvɛnlist]

I'm looking for ...	**Jeg leder efter ...** [jɑ ˈleːðə ˈɛftʌ ...]
restroom	**toilet** [toaˈlɛt]
ATM	**udbetalingsautomat** [uðˀbeˈtæˀleŋs ɑwtoˈmæˀt]
pharmacy (drugstore)	**apotek** [ɑpoˈteˀk]
hospital	**hospital** [hɔspiˈtæˀl]
police station	**politistation** [poliˈti staˈɕoˀn]
subway	**metro** [ˈmeːtʁo]

taxi	**taxi** ['tɑksi]
train station	**togstation** ['tɔw stɑ'ɕoˀn]

My name is ...	**Mit navn er ...** [mit 'nɑwˀn 'æɐ̯ ...]
What's your name?	**Hvad er dit navn?** ['vɑð 'æɐ̯ dit nɑwˀn?]
Could you please help me?	**Kan du hjælpe mig?** ['kan du 'jɛlpə mɑj?]
I've got a problem.	**Jeg har fået et problem.** [ja hɑˀ fɒˀ et pʁo'bleˀm]
I don't feel well.	**Jeg føler mig dårlig.** [ja 'føːlɐ mɑj 'dɒːli]
Call an ambulance!	**Ring efter en ambulance!** ['ʁɛŋə 'ɛftʌ en ɑmbu'lɑŋsə]
May I make a call?	**Må jeg foretage et opkald?** [mɔˀ ja 'fɒːɒˌtæˀ et 'ʌpkalˀ?]

I'm sorry.	**Det er jeg ked af.** [de 'æɐ̯ ja 'keðˀ æˀ]
You're welcome.	**Selv tak.** [sɛlˀ tak]

I, me	**Jeg, mig** [jɑj, mɑj]
you (inform.)	**du** [du]
he	**han** [han]
she	**hun** [hun]
they (masc.)	**de** [di]
they (fem.)	**de** [di]
we	**vi** [vi]
you (pl)	**I, De** [I, di]
you (sg, form.)	**De** [di]

ENTRANCE	**INDGANG** ['enˌgɑŋˀ]
EXIT	**UDGANG** ['uðˌgɑŋˀ]
OUT OF ORDER	**UDE AF DRIFT** ['uːðə æˀ 'dʁɛft]
CLOSED	**LUKKET** ['lɔkəð]

OPEN	**ÅBEN** [ˈɔːbən]
FOR WOMEN	**TIL KVINDER** [te ˈkvenʌ]
FOR MEN	**TIL MÆND** [te ˈmɛnˀ]

MINI DICTIONARY

This section contains 250
useful words required for
everyday communication.
You will find the names of
months and days of the week
here. The dictionary also
contains topics such as colors,
measurements, family, and
more

T&P Books Publishing

DICTIONARY CONTENTS

T&P Books Publishing

time	**tid** (f)	['tið']
hour	**time** (f)	['ti:mə]
half an hour	**en halv time**	[en 'hal' 'ti:mə]
minute	**minut** (i)	[me'nut]
second	**sekund** (i)	[se'kɔn'd]
today (adv)	**i dag**	[i 'dæ']
tomorrow (adv)	**i morgen**	[i 'mɒːɒn]
yesterday (adv)	**i går**	[i 'gɒ']
Monday	**mandag** (f)	['man'da]
Tuesday	**tirsdag** (f)	['tiɡ'sda]
Wednesday	**onsdag** (f)	['ɔn'sda]
Thursday	**torsdag** (f)	['tɒ'sda]
Friday	**fredag** (f)	['fʁɛ'da]
Saturday	**lørdag** (f)	['lœɡda]
Sunday	**søndag** (f)	['sœn'da]
day	**dag** (f)	['dæ']
working day	**arbejdsdag** (f)	['ɑːbɑjds̩dæ']
public holiday	**festdag** (f)	['fɛst̩dæ']
weekend	**weekend** (f)	['wiːˌkɛnd]
week	**uge** (f)	['uːə]
last week (adv)	**sidste uge**	[i 'sistə 'uːə]
next week (adv)	**i næste uge**	[i 'nɛstə 'uːə]
in the morning	**om morgenen**	[ʌm 'mɒːɒnən]
in the afternoon	**om eftermiddagen**	[ʌm 'ɛftʌmeˌdæ'ən]
in the evening	**om aftenen**	[ʌm 'ɑftənən]
tonight (this evening)	**i aften**	[i 'ɑftən]
at night	**om natten**	[ʌm 'natən]
midnight	**midnat** (f)	['miðˌnat]
January	**januar** (f)	['januˌɑ']
February	**februar** (f)	['febʁuˌɑ']
March	**marts** (f)	['mɑːts]
April	**april** (f)	[a'pʁi'l]
May	**maj** (f)	['mɑj']
June	**juni** (f)	['juˀni]
July	**juli** (f)	['juˀli]
August	**august** (f)	[ɑw'gɔst]

September	**september** (f)	[sep'tɛmˀbʌ]
October	**oktober** (f)	[ok'toˀbʌ]
November	**november** (f)	[no'vɛmˀbʌ]
December	**december** (f)	[de'sɛmˀbʌ]

in spring	**om foråret**	[ʌm 'fɒːˌɒˀð]
in summer	**om sommeren**	[ʌm 'sʌmʌən]
in fall	**om efteråret**	[ʌm 'ɛftʌˌɒˀð]
in winter	**om vinteren**	[ʌm 'venˀtʌən]

month	**måned** (f)	['mɔːnəð]
season (summer, etc.)	**årstid** (f)	['ɒːsˌtiðˀ]
year	**år** (i)	['ɒˀ]

2. Numbers. Numerals

0 zero	**nul**	['nɔl]
1 one	**en**	['en]
2 two	**to**	['toˀ]
3 three	**tre**	['tʁɛˀ]
4 four	**fire**	['fiˀʌ]

5 five	**fem**	['fɛmˀ]
6 six	**seks**	['sɛks]
7 seven	**syv**	['sywˀ]
8 eight	**otte**	['ɔːtə]
9 nine	**ni**	['niˀ]
10 ten	**ti**	['tiˀ]

11 eleven	**elleve**	['ɛlvə]
12 twelve	**tolv**	['tʌlˀ]
13 thirteen	**tretten**	['tʁatən]
14 fourteen	**fjorten**	['fjoɐ̯tən]
15 fifteen	**femten**	['fɛmtən]

16 sixteen	**seksten**	['sɑjstən]
17 seventeen	**sytten**	['søtən]
18 eighteen	**atten**	['atən]
19 nineteen	**nitten**	['netən]

20 twenty	**tyve**	['tyːvə]
30 thirty	**tredive**	['tʁaðvə]
40 forty	**fyrre**	['fœɐ̯ʌ]
50 fifty	**halvtreds**	[hal'tʁɛs]

60 sixty	**tres**	['tʁɛs]
70 seventy	**halvfjerds**	[hal'fjæɐ̯s]
80 eighty	**firs**	['fiɐ̯ˀs]
90 ninety	**halvfems**	[hal'fɛmˀs]
100 one hundred	**hundrede**	['hunʌðə]

200 two hundred	**tohundrede**	['tɔw͵hunʌðə]
300 three hundred	**trehundrede**	['tʁɛ͵hunʌðə]
400 four hundred	**firehundrede**	['fiɐ̯͵hunʌðə]
500 five hundred	**femhundrede**	['fɛm͵hunʌðə]

600 six hundred	**sekshundrede**	['sɛks͵hunʌðə]
700 seven hundred	**syvhundrede**	['syw͵hunʌðə]
800 eight hundred	**ottehundrede**	['ɔ:tə͵hunʌðə]
900 nine hundred	**nihundrede**	['ni͵hunʌðə]
1000 one thousand	**tusind**	['tuˀsən]

| 10000 ten thousand | **titusind** | ['ti͵tuˀsən] |
| one hundred thousand | **hundredetusind** | ['hunʌðə͵tuˀsən] |

| million | **million** (f) | [mili'oˀn] |
| billion | **milliard** (f) | [mili'ɑˀd] |

3. Humans. Family

man (adult male)	**mand** (f)	['manˀ]
young man	**ung mand, yngling** (f)	['ɔŋ manˀ], ['øŋleŋ]
woman	**kvinde** (f)	['kvenə]
girl (young woman)	**pige** (f)	['pi:ə]
old man	**gammel mand** (f)	['gaməl 'manˀ]
old woman	**gammel dame** (f)	['gaməl 'dæ:mə]

mother	**mor** (f), **moder** (f)	['moɐ̯], ['mo:ðʌ]
father	**far** (f), **fader** (f)	['fɑ:], ['fæ:ðʌ]
son	**søn** (f)	['sœn]
daughter	**datter** (f)	['datʌ]
brother	**bror** (f)	['bʁoɐ̯]
sister	**søster** (f)	['søstʌ]

parents	**forældre** (pl)	[fʌ'ɛlˀdʁʌ]
child	**barn** (i)	['bɑˀn]
children	**børn** (pl)	['bœɐ̯ˀn]
stepmother	**stedmor** (f)	['stɛð͵moɐ̯]
stepfather	**stedfar** (f)	['stɛð͵fɑ:]

grandmother	**bedstemor** (f)	['bɛstə͵moɐ̯]
grandfather	**bedstefar** (f)	['bɛstə͵fɑ:]
grandson	**barnebarn** (i)	['bɑ:nə͵bɑˀn]
granddaughter	**barnebarn** (i)	['bɑ:nə͵bɑˀn]
grandchildren	**børnebørn** (pl)	['bœɐ̯nə͵bœɐ̯ˀn]

uncle	**onkel** (f)	['ɔŋˀkəl]
aunt	**tante** (f)	['tantə]
nephew	**nevø** (f)	[ne'vø]
niece	**niece** (f)	[ni'ɛ:sə]
wife	**kone** (f)	['ko:nə]

husband	mand (f)	['man']
married (masc.)	gift	['gift]
married (fem.)	gift	['gift]
widow	enke (f)	['ɛŋkə]
widower	enkemand (f)	['ɛŋkə‚man']

name (first name)	navn (i)	['nɑw'n]
surname (last name)	efternavn (i)	['ɛftʌ‚nɑw'n]

relative	slægtning (f)	['slɛgtnɛŋ]
friend (masc.)	ven (f)	['vɛn]
friendship	venskab (i)	['vɛn‚skæ'b]

partner	partner (f)	['pɑ:tnʌ]
superior (n)	overordnet (f)	['ɒwʌ‚ɒ'dnəð]
colleague	kollega (f)	[ko'le:ga]
neighbors	naboer (pl)	['næ:bo'ʌ]

4. Human body

body	krop (f)	['kʁʌp]
heart	hjerte (i)	['jæɐtə]
blood	blod (i)	['blo'ð]
brain	hjerne (f)	['jæɐnə]

bone	ben (i)	['be'n]
spine (backbone)	rygrad (f)	['ʁɒɛg‚ʁɑ'ð]
rib	ribben (i)	['ʁi‚be'n]
lungs	lunger (f pl)	['lɒŋʌ]
skin	hud (f)	['huð']

head	hoved (i)	['ho:əð]
face	ansigt (i)	['ansegt]
nose	næse (f)	['nɛ:sə]
forehead	pande (f)	['panə]
cheek	kind (f)	['ken']

mouth	mund (f)	['mɔn']
tongue	tunge (f)	['tɔŋə]
tooth	tand (f)	['tan']
lips	læber (f pl)	['lɛ:bʌ]
chin	hage (f)	['hæ:jə]

ear	øre (i)	['ø:ʌ]
neck	hals (f)	['hal's]
eye	øje (i)	['ʌjə]
pupil	pupil (f)	[pu'pil']
eyebrow	øjenbryn (i)	['ʌjən‚bʁy'n]
eyelash	øjenvippe (f)	['ʌjən‚vepə]
hair	hår (i pl)	['hɒ']

hairstyle	frisure (f)	[fʁi'sy'ʌ]
mustache	moustache (f)	[mu'stæːɕ]
beard	skæg (i)	['skɛˀg]
to have (a beard, etc.)	at have	[ʌ 'hæːvə]
bald (adj)	skaldet	['skaləð]

hand	hånd (f)	['hʌnˀ]
arm	arm (f)	['aˀm]
finger	finger (f)	['feŋˀʌ]
nail	negl (f)	['najˀl]
palm	håndflade (f)	['hʌnˌflæːðə]

shoulder	skulder (f)	['skulʌ]
leg	ben (i)	['beˀn]
knee	knæ (i)	['knɛˀ]
heel	hæl (f)	['hɛˀl]
back	ryg (f)	['ʁœg]

5. Clothing. Personal accessories

clothes	tøj (i), klæder (i pl)	['tʌj], ['klɛːðʌ]
coat (overcoat)	frakke (f)	['fʁakə]
fur coat	pels (f), pelskåbe (f)	['pɛlˀs], ['pɛlsˌkɔːbə]
jacket (e.g., leather ~)	jakke (f)	['jakə]
raincoat (trenchcoat, etc.)	regnfrakke (f)	['ʁajnˌfʁakə]

shirt (button shirt)	skjorte (f)	['skjoɐ̯tə]
pants	bukser (pl)	['boksʌ]
suit jacket	jakke (f)	['jakə]
suit	jakkesæt (i)	['jakəˌsɛt]

dress (frock)	kjole (f)	['kjoːlə]
skirt	nederdel (f)	['neðʌˌdeˀl]
T-shirt	t-shirt (f)	['tiːˌɕœːt]
bathrobe	badekåbe (f)	['bæːðəˌkɔːbə]
pajamas	pyjamas (f)	[py'jæːmas]
workwear	arbejdstøj (i)	['ɑːbajdsˌtʌj]

underwear	undertøj (i)	['ɔnʌˌtʌj]
socks	sokker (f pl)	['sʌkʌ]
bra	bh (f), brystholder (f)	[be'hɔˀ], ['bʁœstˌhʌlˀʌ]
pantyhose	strømpebukser (pl)	['stʁœmbəˌboksʌ]
stockings (thigh highs)	strømper (f pl)	['stʁœmpʌ]
bathing suit	badedragt (f)	['bæːðəˌdʁagt]

hat	hue (f)	['huːə]
footwear	sko (f)	['skoˀ]
boots (e.g., cowboy ~)	støvler (f pl)	['støwlʌ]
heel	hæl (f)	['hɛˀl]
shoestring	snøre (f)	['snœːʌ]

shoe polish	skocreme (f)	['skoˌkʁɛʔm]
gloves	handsker (f pl)	['hanskʌ]
mittens	vanter (f pl)	['vanʔtʌ]
scarf (muffler)	halstørklæde (i)	['hals 'tœɐ̯ˌklɛ:ðə]
glasses (eyeglasses)	briller (pl)	['bʁɛlʌ]
umbrella	paraply (f)	[paɑ'plyʔ]

tie (necktie)	slips (i)	['sleps]
handkerchief	lommetørklæde (i)	['lʌməˌtœɐ̯klɛ:ðə]
comb	kam (f)	['kɑmʔ]
hairbrush	hårbørste (f)	['hɒˌbœɐ̯stə]

buckle	spænde (i)	['spɛnə]
belt	bælte (i)	['bɛltə]
purse	dametaske (f)	['dæ:me:ˌtaskə]

6. House. Apartment

apartment	lejlighed (f)	['lɑjliˌheðʔ]
room	rum, værelse (i)	['ʁɔmʔ], ['væɐ̯ʌlsə]
bedroom	soveværelse (i)	['sɒwəˌvæɐ̯ʌlsə]
dining room	spisestue (f)	['spi:səˌstu:ə]

living room	dagligstue (f)	['dɑwliˌstu:ə]
study (home office)	arbejdsværelse (i)	['ɑ:bɑjdsˌvæɐ̯ʌlsə]
entry room	entre (f), forstue (f)	[aŋ'tʁɛ], ['fɒˌstu:ə]
bathroom (room with a bath or shower)	badeværelse (i)	['bæ:ðəˌvæɐ̯ʌlsə]
half bath	toilet (i)	[toa'lɛt]

vacuum cleaner	støvsuger (f)	['støwˌsuʔʌ]
mop	moppe (f)	['mʌpə]
dust cloth	klud (f)	['kluðʔ]
short broom	fejekost (f)	['fɑjəˌkɔst]
dustpan	fejeblad (i)	['fɑjəˌblɑð]

furniture	møbler (pl)	['møʔblʌ]
table	bord (i)	['boʔɐ̯]
chair	stol (f)	['stoʔl]
armchair	lænestol (f)	['lɛ:nəˌstoʔl]

mirror	spejl (i)	['spɑjʔl]
carpet	tæppe (i)	['tɛpə]
fireplace	pejs (f), kamin (f)	['pɑjʔs], [ka'miʔn]
drapes	gardiner (i pl)	[gɑ'diʔnʌ]
table lamp	bordlampe (f)	['boɐ̯ˌlampə]
chandelier	lysekrone (f)	['lysəˌkʁo:nə]

| kitchen | køkken (i) | ['køkən] |
| gas stove (range) | gaskomfur (i) | ['gasˌkɔm'fuɐ̯ʔ] |

| electric stove | elkomfur (i) | ['ɛlˌkɔm'fuɡ'] |
| microwave oven | mikroovn (f) | ['mikʁoˌɒw'n] |

refrigerator	køleskab (i)	['køːləˌskæ'b]
freezer	fryser (f)	['fʁyːsʌ]
dishwasher	opvaskemaskine (f)	[ʌp'vaskə ma'skiːnə]
faucet	hane (f)	['hæːnə]

meat grinder	kødhakker (f)	['køðˌhɑkʌ]
juicer	juicepresser (f)	['dʒuːsˌpʁasʌ]
toaster	brødrister, toaster (f)	['bʁœðˌʁɛstʌ], ['tɔwstʌ]
mixer	mikser, mixer (f)	['meksʌ]

coffee machine	kaffemaskine (f)	['kɑfə ma'skiːnə]
kettle	kedel (f)	['keðəl]
teapot	tekande (f)	['teˌkanə]

TV set	tv, fjernsyn (i)	['te'ˌve'], ['fjæɡnˌsy'n]
VCR (video recorder)	video (f)	['vi'djo]
iron (e.g., steam ~)	strygejern (i)	['stʁyəˌjæɡ'n]
telephone	telefon (f)	[telə'fo'n]